Emergency Management for Healthcare, Volume II

Emergency Management for Healthcare
Volume 1

Emergency Management for Healthcare, Volume II

Building a Program

Norman Ferrier

BEP

BUSINESS EXPERT PRESS

Leader in applied, concise business books

This book is dedicated to my loving wife and most stalwart supporter—
Jennifer Johnson.

Description

This series of books focuses on highly specialized Emergency Management arrangements for healthcare facilities and organizations. It is designed to assist any healthcare executive with a body of knowledge which permits a transition into the application of emergency management planning and procedures for healthcare facilities and organizations.

This series is intended for both experienced practitioners of both healthcare management and emergency management, and also for students of these two disciplines.

Keywords

emergency; disaster; mass-casualty event; healthcare; hospital; specialty facility; triage; Disaster Plan; Mass Casualty Plan; Evacuation Plan; staff training; university program; critical incident; Command-and-Control; Incident Management System; disaster recovery

Contents

Acknowledgments

No body of knowledge is ever singular, and no book is ever written in isolation. The author wishes to thank the following individuals; friends certainly, but also both colleagues and mentors, for their reviews and critiquing of material, and for their support and guidance in this project:

Eric Dykes, PhD, Professor of Emergency Planning and Disaster Management (retd.), University of Hertfordshire, Hatfield, UK, and Past President, Institute of Civil Protection and Emergency Management, UK.

Gerald Goldberg, PhD, Professor of Psychology, York University, Toronto, Canada.

Daniel Klenow, PhD, Professor of Emergency Management, University of North Dakota, USA.

Margaret Verbeek, CEM, Past President, International Association of Emergency Managers.

How to Use This Series

This series of books is intended to provide the student of emergency management with a comprehensive introduction to the practice of this discipline within the specialized context of a healthcare setting. It deals with the practice of emergency management from the "ground up," introducing all of the basic concepts and skills, but in the context of healthcare settings. Healthcare institutions, such as hospitals and specialty care facilities, by the very nature of their business, operate with variables which are not normally found in the community at large, and therefore, require more attention than normally occurs in community emergency plans. All of the expected subjects will be covered in some degree of detail. Each chapter will focus on a different aspect of emergency management, always within the specialized context. That is not to say that the content would not be applicable in other types of emergency management; in fact, the opposite is quite true. Each chapter contains both theory and practical applications. In terms of chapter organization, in each case the applicable theory will be addressed, followed by examples which are, wherever possible, specific to the healthcare setting. The examples are then followed by the identification of location-specific problems and by the development of appropriate strategies to address and resolve each type of problem identified. Following each chapter's Conclusion, a series of student projects are recommended, each with the intent of developing the student's experience at the application of practical skills. These are followed by a series of multiple-choice questions, intended to provide the student with a knowledge check prior to moving on to the next chapter. Finally, a list of recommended readings, along with citations and end notes for the content of each chapter are included. The author recognizes the fact that we live in an increasingly digital world, and that good textbooks are becoming increasingly expensive and difficult for both students and their learning institutions to acquire. As a result, wherever possible, instructions have been provided in each citation for accessing the appropriate reference information source online. Additionally, wherever possible, the recommended reading list includes instructions to access the entire books digitally. This series of books is not just intended for a student audience. Working Emergency Managers in both healthcare settings and in community and government settings will hopefully find this information useful and practical. As a result, the author has attempted to include actual examples of the majority of the document types described in the various chapters of this book. These are available digitally, on a copy-protected website, access to which accompanies this book at the time of sale. The website is formatted to permit the viewing of the documents, but not the printing of those documents, and without the ability to modify the documents in any way. As a major labor-saving device, the reader may purchase a password protected one-year renewable license, which will unlock the content of the website, permitting the full customization of each document to reflect local realities, including specific site locations, local telephone numbers, and even the logo of the reader's institution. In essence, this feature permits the rapid development of a comprehensive Emergency Response Plan, and all of the associated documentation, for any type of hospital or other healthcare institution. Information on obtaining such a license is included on the inside leaf of this book.

Introduction

This series of books is intended to teach the skills which have been traditionally associated with the practice of emergency management. This includes all of the skills involved in the assessment of risk, selection of Command-and-Control models, the writing of an Emergency Plan, the testing of that document by means of various types of exercises, and the development of employee education programs which are intended to strengthen familiarity with the Plan. However, no Emergency Plan is a "blueprint" to guide a community or organization through its successful response to a disaster. Every disaster is different in multiple ways and is extremely complex. If we could simply pre-plan and pre-program every type of emergency response from start to finish successfully, we would be in possession of crystal balls, and the need for Emergency Managers would be minimal.

This series of books differs from other well-written and useful emergency management textbooks in two important respects. Firstly, it will deal exclusively with the practice of emergency management as it should occur specifically within a healthcare setting. Secondly, it will attempt to introduce the use of contemporary mainstream business planning practices to the practice of emergency management; something with the potential to build bridges between the Emergency Manager and the senior executive who has little knowledge or understanding of the subject.

The application of emergency management to a healthcare setting is essential. It can be argued that any healthcare institution is, in fact, a highly specialized community. It can also be argued that virtually every type of service or agency found in a normal community has some type of counterpart within the specialized community of a healthcare setting. It is also important to remember that the vast majority of a community's most vulnerable population will typically be found within some sort of healthcare setting, whether an acute care hospital, a specialty care hospital, or a long-term care facility. In order to mitigate against such vulnerabilities and to protect those who possess them, a certain degree of understanding of the clinical context is required. The clinical context is, in the majority of cases, a substantive source of each individual's vulnerability. This is not to say that the Emergency Manager must be an expert clinician, but they do need to possess an understanding of relevant clinical issues. In emergency management, the best Emergency Manager available cannot simply be "dropped" into a hospital to work, any more than they can do so in an oil refinery, a post-secondary institution, a busy international airport, or any other highly specialized institution.

This series of books will attempt to introduce several new mainstream business and academic concepts into the practice of emergency management. These will include formal Project Management, applied research methodology, Root Cause Analysis, Lean for Healthcare, and Six Sigma. All of these concepts have a potentially valuable contribution to make to the effective practice of emergency management. Of equal importance is the fact that for many years the Emergency Manager has been challenged to affect the types of preparedness and mitigation-driven changes that are required within the organization or the community. Part of this has been the challenge of limited resources and competing priorities, but an equally important aspect of this has been the fact that the Emergency Manager has typically used a skill set and information generation and planning processes which were not truly understood by those to whom they reported, and from whom they required project approval.

These mainstream business and academic processes and techniques are precisely the same ones which are used to train senior executives and CEOs for their own positions. As a result, the information generated is less likely to be misunderstood or minimized in its importance, because it comes from a process which the senior executive knows and uses every working day. This "de-mystifies" the practice and the process of emergency management, giving both the Emergency Manager, and emergency management itself, dramatically increased understanding and credibility, potentially making the Emergency Manager a "key player" and contributor to the management team of any organization in which they work, and far more likely to be regarded as an expertise resource.

CHAPTER 1

Command-and-Control Models

Introduction

The response to any emergency situation can be effective, pro-active, and coordinated, or it may be reactive, poorly controlled, and completely chaotic. The four key factors which most often go awry during any emergency response are Command-and-Control, coordination of resources, communications, and supply chain management.[1] Command-and-Control models in emergency management are derived from a notion of "chaos theory" in the social sciences, in which the disaster introduces disorder, and a strong central authority is required to restore that order.[2] While there are emerging thoughts in the field that this may not be the case in all disasters,[3] it is equally clear that, at least in the healthcare setting, strong central authority has always been the method by which crises, large and small, have been managed, and the concept, therefore, remains applicable.

Command-and-Control models are specifically designed to address each of those issues effectively; freeing those in charge to adopt a pro-active approach to incident response, rather than simply reacting to each adverse event as it occurs. The presence or absence of an effective Command-and-Control model will often be the determining factor in the success or the failure of an emergency response. Not only do such models clarify roles and responsibilities, including who is in charge, but they can provide a highly effective framework for interagency cooperation, information sharing, and coordination of activities and resources.

While there are a number of different Command-and-Control models, they are more similar than they are different.[4] Each model does have its own important features and considerations, and each of these will be examined in some detail. Some of these Command-and-Control models are in more general use, and some are used only within a single jurisdiction. The models included do not provide an exhaustive list; appropriate research will provide the student with other examples. In the interest of brevity, this chapter will focus on those Command-and-Control models which the author feels will be of most use to the Emergency Manager in a healthcare setting, and also those models which are most likely to be encountered in the community context, during a major incident.

This chapter will also explore the similarities between the various models, and how these similarities may be exploited to provide highly effective points of coordination between many different types of agencies, with various roles and missions. The primary concentration will, of course, be on how Command-and-Control is applied in a healthcare setting, but it is equally important for the Emergency Manager in a healthcare setting to understand how things work in other agencies, and in the community at large, as these provide the context in which the healthcare institution must operate during any emergency.

Learning Objectives

Upon completion of this chapter, the student should be able to describe the various types of Command-and-Control models in common use in the healthcare setting, as well as in the community at large. The student should be able to describe the key components of each different system, along with its relative strengths and weaknesses. The student should be able to discuss the specific key features which are incorporated into each of the Command-and-Control models which have been discussed. Finally, the student should be able to describe the interoperability of the various models, and how agencies using different models can integrate and coordinate their response activities.

Command-and-Control Models

A Command-and-Control model is a standardized method of controlling and directing the activities of a complex and variable set of resources, in order to address and achieve a specific set of objectives. The specific features of such models may vary somewhat, however, like many other systems which touch on the practice of emergency management, most Command-and-Control models have their origins in the military. They were originally designed to enable military officers to rapidly address the immediate needs of the military unit which they were commanding. As an added bonus, with all officers using the same model, it was remarkably easy to coordinate the activities of multiple individual units, and even single resources, through the use of the model. For those with prior military service, the Command-and-Control models used throughout emergency management will look remarkably similar to what you once knew as "Headquarters Company."

Most models establish a given set of priorities, specifically identifying who is in charge, and also the identification and assignment of responsibility for key general categories of issues which must be at least considered and potentially addressed, regardless of the nature of the incident. While specific titles for the participants may vary somewhat, role tags remain remarkably consistent from one model to the next; while some may be called "Chiefs" and others "Coordinators," "Safety" is always "Safety," "Logistics" remains "Logistics," and so on. Command-and-Control models also establish processes for communications, and also for information gathering, sharing, analysis, and planning. An effective Command-and-Control model will also ensure that needed resources are distributed effectively, that the distribution process is tracked, and that the entire process of response to the emergency, and all of the associated decisions and actions are suitably documented for future study and analysis.

Central to this approach to event management is the use of a regular cycle of meetings, usually called a Business Cycle meeting. Those with key responsibilities will rarely attempt to manage an event by "remote control" from a fixed location; almost all will have pressing issues which need to be addressed in locations other than the Command Center, and the "remote control" approach generally produces results which are less than optimal, in any case. What IS required is an agreement by all of those with key responsibilities, to come together at regular intervals to report progress, to identify problems and problem-solve, to advise the person in charge, and to receive new work direction. Such meetings, when conducted correctly, tend to be high level affairs, with large amounts of useful information and minimal minutia involved.

Such meetings are normally well-structured, of relatively short duration, and manage the information almost as a series of "bullet-points." The frequency and duration of such meetings is normally set by the person in charge and is variable according to the needs of the incident. All such meetings are minute-ed for future use, and progress and problems are typically reported externally at the conclusion of each meeting, using a document called a Situation Report[5] or "Sitrep," completed by person in charge. Copies of sample templates for the documents mentioned in this chapter are available in Microsoft Word format on the webpage, which accompanies this book.

Also, central to this process is the use of Project Planning skills, although many Emergency Managers may not have previously considered this. While the earliest stages of response will be reactive, as control is asserted, the person in charge, if they are wise, will develop a formal document, known as an Incident Action Plan,[6] at the earliest opportunity. It may exist in the earliest stages only in the mind of the person in charge, but should evolve into a formal written document as soon as possible, in order to ensure continuity of the response.

An Incident Action Plan is essentially a formal Project Plan for the management of a crisis, complete with timelines, resource requirements, work assignments, reporting and monitoring processes, benchmarks, and a critical path. About the only things normally found in a Project Plan which are likely to be absent are the Project Charter and the Terms of Reference, which in this case are implicit. While this approach to the management of an emergency has rarely been specifically taught in this manner, the approach and process are immediately recognizable by any project management professional.

Such models will vary somewhat in precisely how the Command-and-Control structure are staffed. Some models have relatively rigid requirements for the staffing of a minimal number of positions, while others are more relaxed, investing all authority in the person in charge, and permitting them to delegate that authority (but not responsibility) to others as and when required, and discontinuing the staffing of positions which are no longer required. A good Command-and-Control structure has predesignated individuals to staff-specific roles, based upon their expertise. A better structure will incorporate multiple layers of redundancy, with several individuals predesignated to staff-specific roles, permitting the depth to address unavailable individuals, and to provide for both around the clock and extended operations. The best structure not only incorporates both of these features but also provides mechanisms for the short-term use of "ad-hoc" staff, thereby enabling the Command-and-Control structure to rapidly activate and to commence operations, even outside of normal business hours, when predesignated staff may have a delayed response.

The best of such models will recognize that one of the greatest challenges to a Command-and-Control model is the ability to safely exceed the written instructions provided, when required. Every Emergency Plan includes a process for activation and one for standing down the response; the true challenge is whether the model employed will be fluid enough and flexible enough to address everything which happens in between. The key to this is the development of an effective team which is suitably experienced in both the management of emergencies, and in the operation of the Command-and-Control model. The best way to achieve this is through regular training and through regular practice sessions, such as exercises, during which the members of the team become accustomed to the model, accustomed to working together, aware of each team members' abilities and knowledge, and sufficiently experienced. The provision of such training, including the creation and staging of exercises, is generally the responsibility of the Emergency Manager. Each of the various models will now be examined individually.

Incident Command System

History

The Incident Command System (ICS) has its origins in the fire services in the immediate vicinity of Phoenix, Arizona, during the late 1960s. It was originally intended as a purely fire service model, called the Fireground Control System, and was intended to coordinate the activities

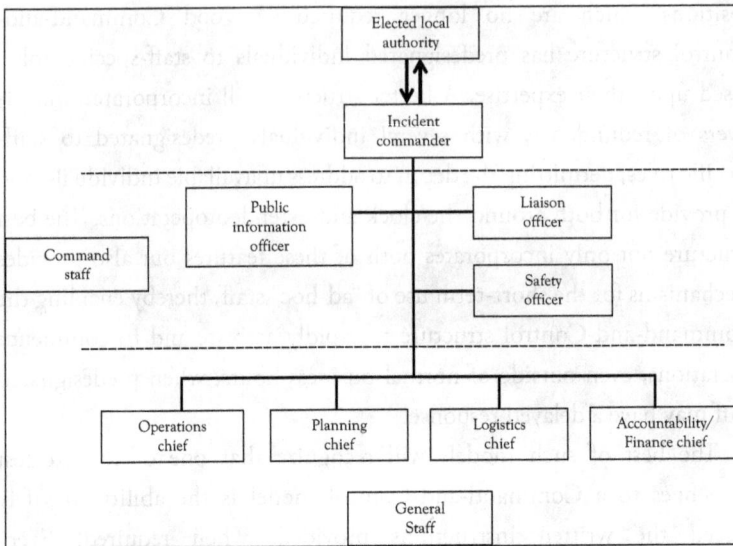

Figure 1.1 Basic incident command system structure

of fire service personnel and resources during major fires. Following a particularly catastrophic wildland fire in southern California during 1970, the model was introduced, in order to attempt to remedy fundamental problems in Command-and-Control, communications, coordination of resources, and supply chains which had been experienced. The model, by now called the ICS, was widely accepted by the fire service in California, and its use began to spread to fire services across the United States. It would eventually become an almost worldwide standard for fire service operations.

The other two "red light" (in the UK and elsewhere, "blue light") services, Police and EMS, were quick to identify potential opportunities arising from the use of ICS by their own organizations. These included not only improved on scene communication and resource management but also an improved ability to coordinate activities between themselves and the other emergency services. As the use of the model grew, other services, particularly those operated by state and municipal governments, including transit, social services, and some healthcare providers, also began to use the model.

The use of the model has slowly spread outside of the fire service in many locations around the world, driven by the need to effectively coordinate activities on an inter-agency level. In 2003, the model became an official national model in the United States, as the Department of Homeland Security mandated its use by emergency services, as a condition of Federal preparedness funding.[7] The model has also been widely accepted across Canada and the UK, with local national variants in use in Australia and New Zealand. The United Nations has also recommended ICS as an international standard for major incident response.[8]

Normal Operations

Most fire services use this model on virtually every response to an emergency. The use of the model begins with an assessment of the situation as it presents, normally called a "size-up," a decision as to the resources required, and a decision as to who will take charge of the incident (Incident Commander). In most services, the incident is then named (e.g., "Maple Street Command") in order to eliminate confusion with other incidents, which may be ongoing simultaneously, and this information is communicated to all incoming resources. As the resources become available, the Command-and-Control model (see Figure 1.1) is implemented, and the response to the incident begins. The response to the incident will be planned and organized, with specific tasks assigned to specific resources, as well as goals and objectives to be met, and all of these will be coordinated by the Incident Commander, by means of a consistent reporting and assessment structure. The model will continue to operate until the incident is resolved, at which point it will be discontinued ("Termination of Command"), and this too will be announced to all present.

Special Functions

Plain Language Communications: All services and organizations responding to the incident will employ a standardized set of terminology for resources, and apart from that, will communicate in plain English, rather than resorting to their own "jargon." To illustrate, a situation which is described in one service's jargon, may have a completely different meaning for another type of service. To illustrate, when an individual is "arrested," the meaning is completely different for a police officer and a paramedic! This feature is intended to recognize that the use of individual types of jargon can sometimes create confusion as to meaning and intent and may even represent an outright barrier to effective communication. In fact, rather than simply eliminating the use of all types of jargon, the use of the model has replaced these with a standardized jargon set, which is intended for use by all services during the coordinated response. This works extremely well in some respects, such as the standardization of key roles, but has varying degrees of success in others, particularly since the standard jargon set remains very fire service-centric, creating its own disconnects for organizations such as hospitals.

Span of Control: Each individual performing a specific function in the model should ideally have only three to seven subordinate reporting resources, with five subordinate resources being optimal. Any number which is less than three should be considered for addition to another reporting structure, or for treatment as an individual resource. Any structure which exceeds seven is in danger of becoming too cumbersome to manage effectively, and that danger increases proportionately with the size of the reporting structure.

Modular Organization: The size and composition of the Command-and-Control structure is flexible and adaptable, based upon the needs of the incident. It can become as large or as small as is required to manage the incident effectively. Resources and roles may not be initially activated, but then activated once the need for each is identified. Resources and roles may be "stood down" when they are no longer required for the management of the incident. In actual practice, many organizations, particularly the emergency services, tend to initially activate the entire structure, paring away unneeded portions as the incident evolves. This is a basic element of the "culture" of most emergency services and reflects the basic premise that it is better to over-respond to an emergency initially and then send unneeded resources away, than to under-respond, and then discover that your resources are insufficient.

Unity of Command: Every individual operating on the site of the emergency has a single individual to whom they report and are accountable.

This is intended to eliminate situations in which staff receives conflicting directions from multiple supervisors.

Coordination: The model is intended to create a bridge for coordination between organizations which do not share a common command structure, or which work together only sporadically, or even rarely. There are a number of available approaches to this feature. In many cases, a single organization will take charge of the overall response, providing some level of direction to the other participating agencies through a single Incident Commander. In some applications, the person in command may move from one organization to another, based upon the needs and expertise available at that particular stage of the incident. To illustrate, during a response to a major traffic accident with multiple victims, fire assumes command until the scene is rendered safe and the access to the victims has been provided, at which point EMS assumes control, for the purpose of the treatment and removal to care of the victims, and when this has occurred, the police assume control for the purpose of investigating the accident and the restoration of normal traffic flow. In the British version of the model, each organization retains their own Incident Commander ("Gold Command") and the multiple Commanders coordinate their activities and work direction among themselves in order to generate consistency. Such models tend to have varying degrees of success at coordination, largely dependent upon pre-existing trust and working relationships. They may not work well when the organizations involved are unaccustomed to working together.[9]

Management by Objectives: The management of the incident is directed at the achievement of specific objectives, or of sets of objectives. These objectives should be a clear and well-understood as possible, should be achievable, and, where possible, should include both priorities for completion and timeframes. This approach is completely consistent with the concept of using the skills of Project Management as a method of managing major incidents.

Incident Action Plan: This model was the first to advocate the development of a formal, written plan for the resolution of each incident.

While the plan may exist only in the mind of the Incident Commander during the earliest stages of the response, it will evolve into a written document. This document outlines strategies for response, goals and objectives, the assignment of specific tasks, and the development of both benchmarks and methods for monitoring progress toward incident resolution. The experienced Emergency Manager will see how this approach treats the resolution of the incident as a project, and actually employs Project Management skills.

Integrated Communications: All of those who participate in an incident response should ideally be a part of a common communications plan. This plan should ensure that the communications technologies used by the various agencies are fully interoperable, and that all responders have the capacity to communicate with one another at some level, even if only among the leadership of each organization.

Coordinated Resource Management: All assets available for response to an incident must be tracked and accounted for. Resources may include physical assets, such as vehicles, materiel, and personnel, and in each case, the status of each resource in terms of location and availability must be known. Procedures for the ordering, movement, tracking, and recovery of resources should be standardized, and all of these should be documented, in order to ensure that no resource request is overlooked.

Strengths

This model attempts to provide a consistent methodology for response to an incident, which is understood and accepted in advance by all responders.

This model attempts to provide clear lines of authority, standardized chains of command, and reporting structures for use in the response to the incident.

This model attempts to ensure that information sharing is consistent across all responding agencies.

This model attempts to address and resolve all four of the key issues which typically go wrong in any incident response; specifically,

Command-and-Control, communications, coordination of resources, and supply chain management.

This model attempts to eliminate independent, uncoordinated decision making and actions in response to the incident, sometimes called "freelancing."

This model attempts to use many of the features of mainstream management techniques, such as Six Sigma (standardized work), Lean (elimination of waste and duplication), and Project Management (Incident Action Plan), although none of these techniques is directly associated with the model.

The model stresses the importance of the safety of all participants, including responders, victims, and bystanders.

Weaknesses

While this model is clearly the oldest and most developed, it remains extremely "fire service-centric," sometimes posing problems for other agencies attempting to employ it. In attempting, for example, to standardize "jargon," the dominant jargon has become primarily that used in the fighting of wildland fires. The attempt to exclude other types of jargon means that while facilities such as Incident Command Posts, Camps, Bases, and Heli-bases are included, none of these are particularly useful to, for example, a hospital.

The model is fundamentally military in its origins, and continues to embrace a somewhat militaristic approach, including the naming of both resources and roles. The use of terms such as "Commander" and "Chief" and "Officer" remain somewhat alien to those in specific sectors which may have a role to play in the response to an emergency, including not only healthcare but also social services, municipal transit, and public utilities, to name but a few examples. This is one of a number of issues which has led to the development of those specialist ICS variants already described.

The attempt to place all resources under a single, central authority sometimes results in organizations questioning the ability of those in charge to understand their specific issues, or their competence to provide comprehensive work direction to highly specialized organizations which they are not a part of. As a result, it is not uncommon for some sectors to develop their own specialized variants of the ICS model, which can be integrated into the overall response structure, but which remain independent and focused on the specific needs of the specialist organizations. To illustrate, while the ICS has become a national standard for response in the United States, over 6,000 American hospitals plus other types of healthcare facilities, utilize the Hospital ICS, a specialist variant of ICS which meets their specific needs, instead of the main model. A similar situation exists in Canada.

The centralized coordination of the model in multiagency responses tends to work best when there is a pre-established working relationship. Otherwise, issues related to lack of familiarity and trust have been known to develop.

Incident Management System

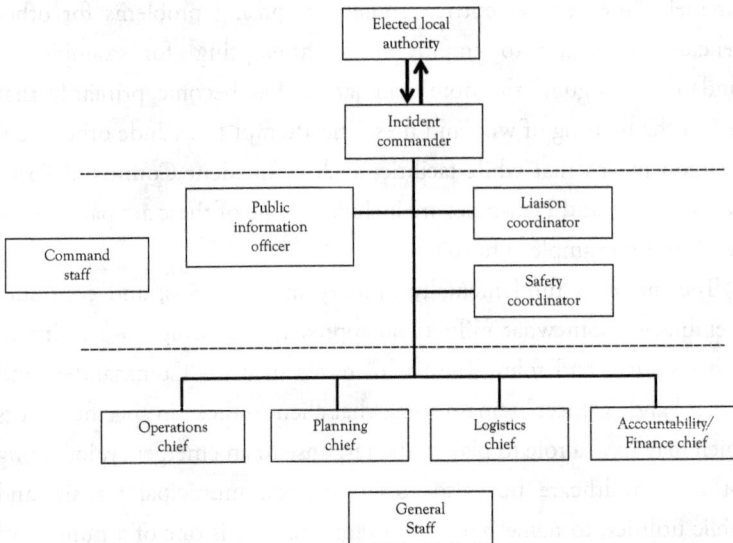

Figure 1.2 Basic incident management system structure

History

The Incident Management System was developed during the 1990s, in an attempt to better meet the specific needs of some sectors of the disaster response community. The model is based directly upon ICS, but it tends to be more flexible and fluid in its approaches to how an incident will be managed. Some of its first applications were in the healthcare and social services sectors, although in some countries, such as Canada, it is rapidly becoming the more widely accepted Command-and-Control model, with ICS being retained for use by many fire services. In the Canadian province of Ontario, the model was first introduced in the jurisdiction's hospitals during 2002, expanding to use by the rest of the response agencies and also those in the private sector, in the province and published as provincial doctrine by Emergency Management Ontario several years later. It continues to grow in popularity, both across Canada around the world, as many agencies see value in its more flexible and less militaristic approach. While its approaches may differ somewhat, the IMS model remains firmly rooted in the ICS from which it originates, and it can be fully integrated within an ICS response model.

Normal Operations

IMS begins with the Incident Manager; all authority and responsibility are initially vested within this position. The Incident Manager is supported by up to seven supporting roles, often referred to as "Key Roles," comprising the Command Staff and the General Staff. These roles are intended to address the seven key issues which every organization must at least consider during its response to any crisis.

The role of the Command Staff is primarily the provision of support to the Incident Manager, taking on responsibilities in order to free the Incident Manager to focus on the actual management of the incident itself. These roles include Public Information (sometimes called Emergency Information) which addresses the needs of the media, Liaison, which is responsible for the sharing and exchange of information with other responder agencies, and Safety, which monitors the safety of all those on the site, stops unsafe work, investigates accidents, and makes recommendations regarding changes to procedures and protective equipment. All of these functions would normally be either the legal responsibility or a legitimate expectation of the Incident Manager.

The role of the General Staff is to provide support to the Incident Manager, but also to participate directly in supporting the physical response to the incident. These roles include Operations, which addresses the core business of the organization, whatever that may be, and also the actual agency response to the incident. Also included is Planning, which is tasked with research and information gathering and analysis affecting the nature of the incident and how well the organization is responding to it. This group also monitors resource use and performs gap analysis. Finally, they assist with the development of short-term (normally less than eight hours), long-term, and recovery planning. Also included is Logistics, which is responsible for the management of resources (both personnel and materiel), sourcing of resources, and the management of supply chains. In some organizations, this role also includes management of the physical plant, and of services (feeding, rest, counselling) required by responders. Finally, it includes Finance/Accountability, which is responsible for both approving required purchases and expanded staffing, and for the tracking of all costs associated with the response to the incident.

It is interesting to note that while the titles have changed in this model, the roles have remained exactly the same. The Commanders and Chiefs and Officers of ICS have been replaced by Managers and Coordinators and Leads or Leaders in IMS. This model has sometimes been described as the "kinder and gentler version of ICS," and its development occurred primarily to address the concerns of some sectors about the "militaristic" nature of the ICS model. While ICS normally staffs all positions in the Command and General Staff during each response, the IMS model places all authority in the Incident Manager, and all other roles become active only when the Incident Manager decides that they are required. They will also be de-activated as soon as the Incident Manager decides that they are no longer needed. In most cases, the Command Staff will primarily support the Incident Manager, while the General Staff will primarily, but not exclusively, support the Operations role.

As in ICS, the Business Cycle Meeting is a central feature of the management model. There is also an expectation that a formal Incident Action Plan, embracing all of the central concepts of Project Management already discussed, will be developed for each incident. Participation in the meetings, along with the duration and frequency of the meetings, are determined at the discretion of the Incident Manager.

All meetings are minute-ed, and reporting requirements and procedures are similar to the ICS model. Examples of the documents mentioned in this chapter are available in Microsoft Word format on the webpage which accompanies this textbook.

Special Functions

Strengths

The model provides a relatively clear division of responsibilities for the subordinate reports of each of the Key Role staff, without filling the Point of Command with individuals in subordinate roles who do not really need to be constantly present.

The model recognizes that every single box does not need to be populated throughout the duration of the incident. This factor permits the Incident Manager to rotate staff out to rest, or to replace idle time in one role with a productive contribution to the incident response in another, more needed role.

The model recognizes that individual agencies and types of organizations must be able to function during a crisis without the introduction of a new and unfamiliar chain of command and respects the existing organizational business model wherever possible. To this end, the Incident Manager and the Key Roles are standardized, while the balance of the organization reports and receives work direction through whichever of the Key Roles which the organization feels best meets their own needs as an organization. To illustrate, some organizations may place site security under Operations, but another may well place the same function under Logistics, if that is where they would normally report in the organization's business model.

While the Incident Manager is likely to be too busy, and the Operations Lead too specialized, the other six Key Role positions provide a highly effective framework for coordination, collaborative planning, and resource sharing, between the home organization and other agencies with which they may not have a robust, ongoing relationship. This is accomplished through role-specific collaboration, in which Logistics may meet regularly with Logistics, Public Information may collaborate on a joint Media Plan, and Planners may regularly share the information which their research has revealed with their counterparts at other agencies.

Weaknesses

In the IMS model, the central authority is not typically as strong, and interagency cooperation tends to be collaborative, rather than having a lead agency simply issue work direction to the others. While this "kinder and gentler" version of Incident Command may be more palatable to the majority of organizations, it can sometimes slow the collaboration process, since individuals are "asked" to perform certain activities, rather than simply being directed to do so.

It has been observed that the reduced rigidity of this model forces each Incident Manager to rely on leadership skills and team building, rather than lines of authority and chains of command.

Australasian Inter-Service Incident Management System

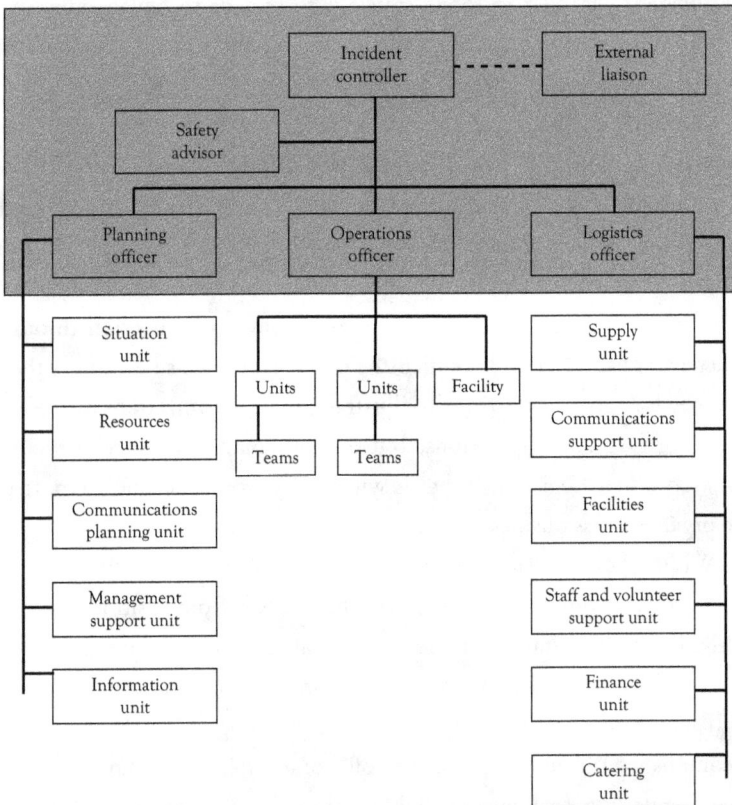

Figure 1.3 Basic Australasian Inter-Service Incident Management System

History

The Australasian Inter-Service Incident Management System (AIIMS) is the national incident management model in Australia. It was created during 1989 by the Australian Association of Rural Fire Authorities and is derived directly from the generic Incident Management System model. The model is copyrighted, and that copyright is held by the Australian Fire and Emergency Service Authorities Council.[10] The model is derived directly from the generic ICS, with changes in structure and in terminology which better reflected existing Australian Command-and-Control.[11] The model has been successfully deployed in numerous major incidents, including wildland fires, floods, and tropical cyclones, to name just a few.[12] The model is intended for application in any inter-agency response, within the context of the specific legislation governing each participating agency or intended to address the type of incident being responded to.

Normal Operations

During normal operations an Incident Controller will be appointed during the early stages of any incident. That Incident Controller will then evaluate the situation as it occurs, and then will decide to activate all of the Incident Management Team, or only those members of the team who the Incident Controller feels are actually required. The four members of the Incident Management Team will continue to evaluate, and each will activate those subordinate functions which they feel are required, or which the Incident Controller has directed to be activated. They will collaborate to determine a specific set of objectives, as well as an Incident Action Plan for the resolution of the incident, and this information will be communicated to all of those who are responding to the incident, in order to ensure consistency of purpose.

There are clear lines of communications, with every person responding to the incident reporting to a single person (frontline staff to team leaders, team leaders to Unit Leaders, Unit Leaders to Operations, etc.) and every person having a clear understanding of how they are receiving their work direction and where to take any problems which they encounter. While the generic Incident Management System model proposes the establishment of the model within each of the various agencies responding to the incident, and the use of Key Role staff as potential points of interagency coordination, the AIIMS model proposes a single, integrated Command-and-Control structure, with the command unified by terms of advance agreements between the agencies involved. There are advantages and disadvantages to both approaches. To illustrate, while effecting a change in the response using the AIIMS model is likely to occur more quickly because of a single, unified, Command-and-Control structure, those in the Command-and-Control structures of the mainstream IMS model, being service-specific, are likely to have a much more thorough understanding of the resources, procedures, and issues being addressed by the group which they supervise.

Special Functions

Management by Objectives: The desired outcomes of the incident are determined by the Incident Controller and the Incident Management Team collaboratively and are communicated to all of those who are responding to the incident. At any given time, there can be only one Incident Action Plan, and one set of objectives operating, thereby ensuring that all personnel are working toward the same set of objectives. This facilitates understanding and eliminates potential confusion. As with any Incident Action Plan, this process is highly amenable to the techniques of Project Management.

Functional Management: Specifically, the use of a single set of specific functions to manage an incident. In this case, there are four such functions:

- **Control**—Managing all activities which are required in order to resolve the incident.
- **Planning**—Collection, analysis, dissemination of information, and the creation of any plans required to resolve the incident.
- **Operations**—Assignment and application of those resources required to resolve the incident.

- **Logistics**—Acquiring and distributing all resources, whether human or material, services or facilities, which are required in order to resolve the incident.

Span of Control

The number of resources which can be effectively supervised by a single person. In this model, the proposed "ideal" is five, with the suggestion that the supervisor should consider delegation to someone else when the ideal number is exceeded or might also consider either reassuming responsibility or re-organizing the reporting structure as the incident winds down.

Strengths

This model is intended to strengthen and formalize control and the coordination of operations between the various agencies which are responding to an incident. It is intended to achieve these goals without compromising the internal chains of command of the participating agencies.

The use of a single, unified, Command-and-Control group means that this model is likely to react to any change in situation much more quickly than is the case in other models in which the Command-and-Control structure is essentially duplicated across multiple agencies, and then coordinated through the use of the team members in like roles from various organizations.

The model attempts to standardize communications, primarily through the use of a standardized set of terminology, which has been accepted by and is in use by all of the participating agencies.

This model treats the safety, health, and welfare of the responders of all agencies as priority objectives within the response process, with effective measures and resources in place to ensure that these objectives are met.

This model promotes an approach to incident management which is adaptable, fully scalable, flexible, and fluid. Roles and resources are activated only when the Incident Controller determines that they are required. The model is fully adaptable to an incident which is either escalating or decreasing in size, primarily through the assignment of duties and by maintaining a manageable span of control.

This model may be universally applied by any emergency management organization in any setting, provided that the appropriate advance training and operating agreements are in place.

This model promotes economies of both cost and scale, through the use of shared resources and enhanced communications, and through agencies working together in any response setting.

This model is intended to be sufficiently flexible that not all of its roles require a specific background in emergency service operations. While it is likely that the Incident Controller will always be from an emergency services background, nonemergency personnel may be employed in a variety of the required Incident Management Team roles.

Weaknesses

While all of the Key Roles identified in a generic Incident Management System model are present, the relegation of some of these to subordinate roles under one of the defined Incident Management Team positions, may render them more difficult to use as potential points of coordination.

This model has adopted the single set of jargon approach to communications which is found within the generic ICS. As a result, care will be needed to ensure that the jargon set meets all of the needs of all participating agencies, and that any potential service or agency-specific alternate meanings for specific terms (e.g., "arrest" for policeman vs. paramedic) are carefully eliminated.

The use of a single Incident Management Team may result in an incorrect understanding of the resources, capabilities, or issues of an individual agency, which may not be directly represented on the team.

U.S. National Incident Management System

History

The U.S. National Incident Management System (NIMS) is described by the U.S. Federal Emergency Management Administration as a

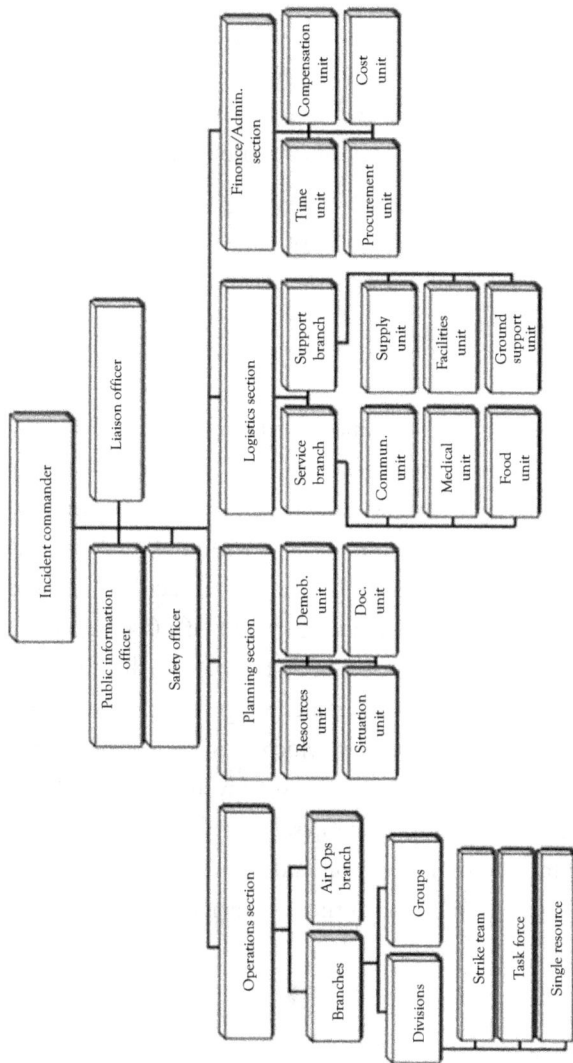

Figure 1.4 Basic U.S. National Incident Management System Example

"comprehensive, systematic, nationwide approach to emergency management."[13] It was an integral part of a sweeping change to the practice of emergency management in the United States, following the horrific events of September 11, 2001. The model has been mandated for use in all U. S. Federal Departments through Homeland Security Presidential Directive #5,[14] which also makes the adoption of the model by state and local governments and for private organizations a mandatory condition for receiving Federal preparedness awards. The Federal Emergency Management Agency offers various types of training in this model, through its training arm, the Emergency Management Institute.[15]

Normal Operations

In this model, the issue of Command-and-Control has been integrated into a multifaceted approach to incident management, as one of five key factors, including preparedness, communications and information management, resource management, command and "management," and ongoing management and maintenance. NIMS incorporates three key components, including the ICS, The Multi-Agency Coordination System, and Public Information.[16] The model mandates the use of the ICS, to the level of Command and General Staffs (see Figure 1.1), with organization and assignment of specific tasks below those levels carrying some degree of flexibility (see example in Figure 1.4). The Multi-Agency Coordination System is a process which is intended to allow all levels of government to work together during any incident. It also provides coordination across various disciplines. The Public Information function also receives mandatory integration and coordination across all levels of government and organizations during any incident.

Special Functions

This model is intended to provide a standardized approach to incident management which is both flexible and scalable, as required by the nature of the incident.

This model is intended to enhance cooperation and interoperability among responders.

This model is intended to provide efficient resource coordination among jurisdictions and organizations.

Strengths

This model strives to provide a level of coordination and resource sharing which has never before been experienced in incident management.

This model has combined most of the previous proposed approaches into a fully integrated system.

Weaknesses

The model is both large and complex, and it requires training to be utilized correctly. The challenge will be in providing that training to the vast numbers of people who will need to have it, particularly in the face of conflicting demands for limited resources.

There are key sectors, specifically healthcare and social services, which are likely to be initially resistant to the military character of the Command-and-Control model.

While there is some familiarity with certain elements of this model, specifically ICS, it incorporates a sufficient number of changes to necessitate a good deal of ongoing exercise play in order to truly make it the "new normal" in the minds of all involved.

History

This system attempts to identify and to isolate each of the critical components of response to a disaster situation, and to assign the responsibility for the leadership of each to a specific person or organization, as well as designating any other organizations required to play supporting roles in the provision of services associated with that Emergency Support Function (ESF). The assignment of responsibility for each will vary, according to the level of government employing the model. To illustrate, the U.S. Federal government designates Federal agencies for leadership and supporting roles in each ESF, but at the local level, the responsibility might be assigned to a municipal department, a contractor, or even a

ESF#1	Transportation
ESF#2	Communications
ESF#3	Public works and engineering
ESF#4	Firefighting
ESF#5	Emergency management
ESF#6	Mass care, emergency assistance, housing, and human services
ESF#7	Logistics management and resource support
ESF#8	Public health and medical services
ESF#9	Search and rescue
ESF#10	Oil and hazardous materials response
ESF#11	Agriculture and natural resources
ESF #12	Energy
ESF #13	Public safety and security
ESF #14	Long-term community recovery
ESF #15	External affairs

Figure 1.5 Emergency support functions[17]

volunteer group. The most common approach to this is the inclusion in the Emergency Response Plan of an Annex covering the specific information for each of the individual ESFs. The title and structure of each function has been standardized, in order to foster consistency for both communications and usage, across the various levels of government.

The notion of specialized ESFs first appeared in the late 1990s with a model which included 12 designated functions. As of 2013, this number had grown to 15 separate and distinct functions. This model is a component of the U.S. National Incident Management Strategy, along with the ICS. It is also sometimes used by local authorities as an addition to local emergency preparedness arrangements, either in conjunction with ICS or, occasionally, with another Command-and-Control model, and as part of the planning framework for the development of the local community's Emergency Response Plan.

Normal Operations[18]

ESF #1 Transportation: The management of transportation systems and infrastructure, for both people and goods, in response to an actual or potential emergency.

ESF #2 Communications: Supports the restoration of communications infrastructure, coordinates communications support to incident response efforts, and facilitates the delivery of information to emergency management decision makers.

ESF #3 Public Works and Engineering: Assessment of public works and infrastructure, including postincident assessment of structural damage, emergency contract support for lifesaving and life-sustaining services, engineering expertise, construction management, real estate services, and emergency repairs.

ESF #4 Firefighting: Detection and suppression of wildland, rural, and urban fires resulting from, or occurring coincidentally with, an "all-hazard" incident.

ESF #5 Emergency Management: Collects, analyzes, processes, and disseminates information about a potential or actual incident and conducts planning activities to facilitate the overall activities in providing assistance to the whole community.

ESF #6 Mass Care, Emergency Assistance, Housing, and Human Services: Coordinates and provides life-sustaining resources, essential services, and statutory programs, including emergency shelter, temporary housing, and mass-feeding.

ESF #7 Logistics Management and Resource Support: Logistics integrates whole community logistics incident planning and support for timely and efficient delivery of supplies, equipment, services, and facilities.

ESF #8 Public Health and Medical Services: Public health, healthcare delivery, and emergency response systems to minimize and/or prevent health emergencies from occurring, detect and characterize health incidents, provide medical care and human services to those affected, reduce the public health and human service effects on the community, and enhance community resiliency to respond to a disaster.

ESF #9 Search and Rescue: Distress monitoring, incident communications, locating distressed personnel, coordination, and execution of rescue operations, including extrication and/or evacuation, along with providing medical assistance and civilian services through the use of public and private resources to assist persons.

ESF #10 Oil and Hazardous Materials Response: Responds to a threat to public health, welfare, or the environment caused by actual or potential oil and hazardous materials incidents.

ESF #11 Agriculture and Natural Resources: Provides nutrition assistance; responds to animal and agricultural health issues; provides technical expertise, coordination, and support of animal and agricultural emergency management.

ESF #12 Energy: Facilitates the reestablishment of damaged energy systems and components.

ESF #13 Public Safety and Security: Provides law-enforcement and supports law-enforcement activities.

ESF #14 Long-Term Community Recovery: Coordinates efforts aimed at disaster recovery and the restoration of normal or "near-normal" status to the community. Continues to be common at the local level but is often superseded at the Federal level by the U.S. National Disaster Recovery Framework.

ESF #15 External Affairs: Provides accurate, coordinated, timely, and accessible information to affected audiences, including governments, media, the private sector, and the local populace.

Special Functions

This system is not, strictly speaking, a Command-and-Control model, although it is occasionally presented as such, particularly by both communities and organizations which have not formally adopted an actual formal Command-and-Control model (e.g., "The Mayor is in charge, assisted by the Council, and the Fire Chief will control the scene"). While all of the ESFs are functional at the Federal and State levels, some may have limited application at the community or organizational levels. With these provisos, the model is a very useful planning and preparedness tool.

Strengths

While not actually a formal Command-and-Control model, this model, nonetheless, performs an exceptional response to the "age-old" discussion in emergency management circles about exactly who does what. It provides clear assignment of responsibility, levels of responsibility, and scopes of operations.

Weaknesses

This model lacks a formal command structure. In particular, it does not address the question of who is in charge. It also creates an organizational structure which may be too large and cumbersome to function as an actual command team.

The model also encounters occasional problems with the agencies primarily responsible for each ESF in obtaining both information and resources from other agencies, which may or may not be an intended part of the response apparatus.[19]

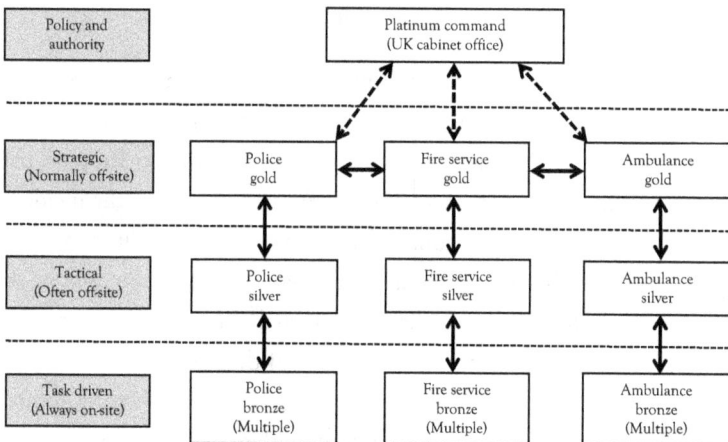

Figure 1.6 UK Gold, Silver, Bronze System

UK Gold, Silver, Bronze System

History

This model was created in 1985 by the London Metropolitan Police. It was created following a serious riot which occurred in North London during which serious disconnects in communications occurred. The riot ultimately resulted in the death of a uniformed police constable. A team, led by then-Inspector Peter Power, determined that there were three essential roles, Strategic, Tactical, and Operational Command, which needed to operate in such situations; roles which were more important than the actual ranks of the officers.[20] These were ultimately named Gold, Silver, and Bronze, and each was directly subordinate to the other, with Gold at the top of the hierarchy. The model was quickly adopted by the various UK police services and spread from there to the other two "blue light" services, fire and ambulance. It is the single recognized standard for Command-and-Control in the UK and was recognized legislatively through the UK's Civil Contingencies Act of 2004.[21] The model is now in mandatory use in the UK by all Category One responders (local authorities, police, fire, ambulance, Coast Guard, Environment Agency, National Health Service Trusts, etc.) and in widespread use among Category Two responders (primarily, but not exclusively, privately held corporate entities, providing services in the Energy, Communications, and Transportation sectors).[22]

Normal Operations

Under normal circumstances, the model is intended to "roll out" the aforementioned roles during major incidents. These roles include the formulation of strategy, implementation of tactics to support that strategy, and the actual tasks which were required to resolve the incident, also referred to as Operational Command. They are intended for implementation without a great deal of consideration of the rank of the person holding the position, although in actual practice the roles tend to ultimately resolve themselves along the lines of the normal organizational ranks of those involved. Gold Command (Strategy) is usually located off-scene. In some cases, the Gold Commanders of the various services will be co-located but may also confer via videoconferencing. Silver

Commanders (Tactical) may operate on scene but are also frequently providing supporting services and direction from an off-scene location. Bronze Commanders (Operational) provide work direction to frontline staff, almost exclusively on the scene of the incident.[23]

Special Functions

A fourth level, sometimes called "Platinum" is occasionally used to identify those who actually provide the policy framework and authorization for the activities of the three subordinate roles. This level is usually attributed to the emergency apparatus of the UK Cabinet, using the exotic-sounding acronym "COBRA" (Cabinet Office Briefing Room, originally always Briefing Room "A"), although the use of the term "Platinum" has not been universally or formally adopted, and remains the subject of some debate.

Strengths

This model relies on pre-existing, established chains of command and lines of communication. Staff does not have to receive work direction from unfamiliar sources during a crisis.

Weaknesses

The vast majority of coordination occurs at the Gold level, which makes the individual service participants relatively insular.

Communications and coordination between frontline staff may potentially being occurring without the knowledge of the various Gold Commanders.

There appears to be no formal provision for task-level, multiservice operating groups, such as the Task Force groups which are an option in the USNIMS model.

Conclusion

There are many Command-and-Control models in use in various communities around the world. While there are, at first glance, fundamental differences between the various Command-and-Control models, with detailed examination it becomes evident that these models are fundamentally more similar than dissimilar. While many of these models have now spread across entire business sectors and even countries, it must be remembered that each model was originally developed in order to meet the coordination needs of a specific organization or region. As a result, many Command-and-Control models contain "legacy" features which, while useful to the parent organization, may be of less use to other adopting organizations, and may actually, in some cases, pose barriers to their use for some organizations.

With this is mind, there are really only so many "correct" approaches to Command-and-Control, and, as a result, once the user sifts through the jargon, and considers the various roles which are included in the organization chart of each model as generic functions, all of the models examined here, and many of the others omitted in the interest of brevity, possess fundamental commonalities. It must always be remembered that the primary function of any Command-and-Control model is the ability to control, direct, communicate with, and supply one's own resources. Interagency coordination is an ideal outcome, but not necessarily an essential one. In fact, many organizations may feel that they are so specialized in the nature of their work that too much external direction is counterproductive, or even dangerous in some cases. The healthcare sector would be a good example of this, and this perception, whether correct or erroneous, has driven the development of a number of sector-specific Command-and-Control models.

All Command-and-Control models, whether generic or specialized, must possess certain critical features which permit some level of cross-agency communications and coordination to occur. These include operating levels which include policy, strategy, tactics and task-driven operational levels, and the similar labelling of roles. Whether one is called a Chief, an Officer, or a Coordinator, the functional label of "Logistics" should always remain "Logistics," and so on.

Some issues, such as the validity of any attempt at a broad standardization of resource names across such a diverse group of organizations, or an attempt to centralize the Command-and-Control of highly specialized operations by individuals who, while well intentioned and knowledgeable about emergency response do not fully understand the core business of the specialty organization, may pose more problems than they are intending to solve, but this remains open to debate. These realities remain true in most of the Command-and-Control models in use around the world, and they are certainly true among these examples.

Having examined this sampling of generic and "mainstream" models, the next chapter will focus on the examination of Command-and-Control models which have been developed specifically to meet the needs of the healthcare sector. For the Emergency Manager operating in a healthcare setting, the challenge is always to choose a Command-and-Control model which best meets the specialized needs of your own organization, and which can ideally be integrated smoothly into the Command-and-Control models of the other organizations in the community.

Student Projects

Student Project #1

Prepare a formal report comparing and contrasting the structure and features of the U.S. NIMS and the AIIMS. Discuss what are in your opinion the strengths and the weaknesses of each model and defend these opinions. Ensure that the information contained in your report is suitably cited and referenced in order to demonstrate that an appropriate level of research has occurred.

Student Project #2

Prepare a formal report comparing and contrasting the structure and features of the generic ICS and the British Gold, Silver, Bronze System. Discuss what are in your opinion the strengths and the weaknesses of each model and defend these opinions. Ensure that the information contained in your report is suitably cited and referenced in order to demonstrate that an appropriate level of research has occurred.

Test Your Knowledge

Take your time. Read each question carefully and select the MOST CORRECT answer for each. The correct answers appear at the end of the section. If you score less than 80 percent (eight correct answers) you should re-read this chapter.

1. The ICS has its origins in the State of Arizona, within the:

   (a) Fire Service
   (b) Police Service
   (c) Emergency Medical Service
   (d) Emergency Management Agency

2. The structures and functions of the ICS are based upon similar Command-and-Control models found in the:

   (a) Fire Service
   (b) Military
   (c) Federal Government Agencies
   (d) All of the Above

3. In both the ICS and IMS models, the primary function of the Command Staff is to:

   (a) Ensure that liability exposures are avoided
   (b) Document the response to the incident
   (c) Ease the workload of the Incident Manager
   (d) Ensure the effective functioning of the Point of Command

4. In the Incident Management System model, each Key Role staff position is activated:

   (a) At the start of the incident
   (b) When the Point of Command is activated

(c) As soon as they arrive at the scene

(d) When the Incident Manager determines that the position is required

5. The organizational structure and the operating features of the generic Incident Management System model are based upon those of the:

(a) Australasian Inter-Service Incident Management System
(b) British Gold, Silver, Bronze System
(c) ESFs System
(d) Incident Command System

6. In the British Gold, Silver, Bronze System, each emergency service agency typically functions as an independent entity with its own chain of command, and interagency coordination typically occurs:

(a) Only when required
(b) When authorized by the Platinum level
(c) At the Gold Command level
(d) Among the Bronze Commanders at the incident

7. In the ICS and IMS models, a meeting in which the Incident Commander exchanges information, receives activity reports, and issues new work assignments is called a:

(a) Commander's Meeting
(b) Business Cycle Meeting
(c) Staff Briefing
(d) Reporting Cycle

8. The document created by the Incident Commander/Manager in order to share the current state of operations with senior management, outside agencies and other levels of government is called a:

(a) Situation Report

(b) After Action Report

(c) Incident Commander's Briefing Paper

(d) Any of the Above

9. In the ICS, centralized command tends to have varying degrees of success at coordination, which are largely dependent upon:

(a) Pre-existing trust

(b) Pre-existing working relationships

(c) The strength of the Incident Commander's personality

(d) Both (a) and (b)

10. In the U.S. NIMS the three major components are the ICS, Public Information, and:

(a) The Incident Management System

(b) The Situation Unit

(c) The Multi-Agency Coordination System

(d) The Gold, Silver, Bronze System

Answers

1. (a)   2. (b)   3. (c)   4. (d)   5. (d)

6. (c)   7. (b)   8. (a)   9. (d)   10. (c)

Additional Reading

The author recommends the following exceptionally good titles as supplemental readings, which will help to enhance the student's knowledge of those topics covered in this chapter:

Australian Fire and Emergency Service Authorities Council. 2004. Australasian Inter-Service Incident Management System Manual, .pdf document, http://training.fema.gov/EMIWeb/edu/docs/cem/Comparative%20EM%20-%20Session%2021%20-%20Handout%2021-1%20AIIMS%20Manual.pdf (accessed February 19, 2014).

Farazmand, A. 2001, Handbook of Crisis and Emergency Management, CRC Press, Boca Raton, FL, ISBN: 9781420002454

FEMA National Preparedness Resource Library. www.fema.gov/national-preparedness-resource-library (accessed February 20, 2014).

FEMA. 2014. National Incident Management System: Independent Study Course, Emergency Management Institute, Distance Learning Course, at: http://training.fema.gov/IS/NIMS.aspx (accessed February 21, 2014).

Moore, T and R. Lakha. 2007. Tolley's Handbook of Disaster and Emergency Management, Taylor and Francis, London, ISBN-10 1136355375, ISBN-13: 9781136355370

US FEMA. 2008. Emergency Support Function Annexes: Introduction, U.S. Federal Emergency Management Agency, Washington, .pdf document, www.fema.gov/pdf/emergency/nrf/nrf-esf-intro.pdf (accessed February 19, 2014).

CHAPTER 2

Command and Control for Healthcare

Introduction

In the last chapter, we discussed a variety of what might be called "mainstream" command and control models, including both the Incident Command System (ICS) and the Incident Management System (IMS), and examined how they operated. While these models may work exceedingly well in the community setting, there are fundamental realities which challenge their ability to be fully effective in a hospital or healthcare setting.

Hospitals, for very valid reasons, require their own, specialized, Command and Control systems. Disasters often have both immediate and long-term effects on both population health and on health delivery, in both the developed and the developing world.[1] That being said, the community's Command-and-Control systems do represent the context in which the Command-and-Control systems of the hospitals and healthcare providers will be operating. As a result, while the systems used in healthcare remain specialized, they must also remain fully integrate-able and inter-operable with the mainstream systems.

This chapter will examine the reasons why specialized Command-and-Control models are required in healthcare. We will also examine two healthcare-specific Command-and-Control models: the Hospital Incident Command System (HICS) and the Healthcare Emergency Command and Control System (HECCS). The two models will be examined in detail in both normal and special operations, and their features and also relative strengths and weaknesses will be discussed. Finally, these models will be examined in terms of their interoperability, both with each other, and with the mainstream command and control models likely to be in use in the community.

Learning Objectives

Upon completion of this chapter, the student should be able to discuss the rationale for the use of specialized Command-and-Control models in the hospital and healthcare sector, and why the use of "mainstream" Command-and-Control models often fail to meet the needs of this sector. The student should be able to compare and contrast the structures, features, and operating systems of both the HICS model and the Healthcare HECCS model and discuss the relative strengths and weaknesses of each. Finally, the student should be able to discuss how facilities using these two models may have their models successfully integrated, and also how to integrate the use of either model with the "mainstream" Command-and-Control models, such as ICS or IMS, which are in use in communities.

Why Healthcare Settings Are Different

In the emergency planning practiced in many communities, hospitals are either viewed with a certain degree of mysteriousness, or in the same category as independent businesses operating in the community. In the first case, their roles and abilities as far as emergency management is concerned are mostly a matter of blind faith or sometimes erroneous assumptions. To illustrate, the community Emergency Plan simply states that, in the event that the passenger train which passes through town three times each day ever derails, "the injured will be taken to the hospital." This generates an assumption which essentially ignores the fact that the local hospital probably doesn't have either the capacity or the resources to handle all of those trauma patients,[2] or may be a signatory to a regional hospital programme agreement, in which another hospital, miles away, is the designated receiving location for all trauma patients.

The primary business of every hospital is essentially clinical; everything in the facility can be related in some fashion, either directly or indirectly, to meeting the medical needs of the patients. Additionally, hospitals are arguably, along with long-term care facilities, the single greatest concentrations of truly vulnerable individuals within any community.[3] That vulnerability arises, for the most part, as a direct result of the clinical condition of each patient, and of the medical treatments and procedures which they have received.

The degrees of vulnerability, and the support required, vary as a direct result of clinical situations. To illustrate, it is relatively easy to evacuate a voluntary mental health patient to another facility, whereas a general surgical patient requires more support, and a patient who is freshly post-operative or in the Intensive Care Unit, will require a tremendous amount of support to be safely evacuated. The other two factors which play a major role in influencing evacuation in a hospital are the relative degree of mobility (a MAJOR issue), and, in some cases, the degree of supervision required to ensure patient safety.[4] In general terms, those conducting "mainstream" emergency management or response activities in the community rarely possess an appropriate level of understanding of the clinical issues which drive so many of a healthcare institution's emergency decisions, or even how they operate on a day-to-day basis.

The second case, in which hospitals are essentially independent businesses operating in the community, is equally erroneous. Independent businesses have limited and specialized resource bases, and in a disaster, are likely to be primarily focused on their own survival. Hospitals are specialized, but have a broad resource base, and are focused on the survival of the community, with their own survival being an important secondary consideration.

Most healthcare facilities are truly communities in miniature, although a great deal more specialized in their core business and on a smaller scale. In the Emergency Support Function model, which is described in detail in Chapter 1, of the 15 Emergency Support Functions (ESF) incorporated into the model, only ESF #10 (and increasingly, hospitals are being forced to develop their own internal hazardous materials spill response and decontamination arrangements) and ESF #11 (Agriculture and Natural Resources) do not have analogs operating within the facility. Community police are replaced by hospital security, EMS by the hospital Cardiac Arrest Team, Public Works and Utilities by the Engineering Department, and so on.

Location-Specific Factors

While some locations enjoy a relatively free choice with respect to Command-and-Control model selection, others must meet specific mandates, often legislated. Such systems are generally attempting to ensure that all parties responding to an emergency are using a single, predesignated Command-and-Control model, ensuring coordination. Participation in such systems may be voluntary, but it may also be based on such government strategies as being able to demonstrate compliance in order to access preparedness funding grants. While such systems are both coordinated and interoperable across multiple types of organizations and service providers, they only rarely fully address the specific needs of each type of participating organization or agency from their Command-and-Control model.

In the United States, Federal legislation has mandated that no preparedness grant funding would be available to any agency unless it was fully compliant with the United States. National Incident Management System command and control model,[5] and various sectors, including healthcare, were provided with actual deadlines for compliance. In the United Kingdom, the Gold, Silver, Bronze system has become the accepted standard for command and control, including the healthcare sector.[6] In Australia, Federal legislation mandates the use of the AIIMS model.[7] While such directions are well-intentioned, they are, of necessity, somewhat generic, and only rarely will a participating organization find that they can participate during a crisis without considerable advance consideration of "work-arounds" which will permit the organization to meet its own specific needs, while remaining in compliance.

Such directives may also force organizations with their own specific procedures, chains of command, language, and priorities to suddenly adopt a less familiar Command-and-Control structure during a crisis, with a corresponding degree of potential for confusion to result. The only alternative to this is the provision of fairly extensive and ongoing training initiatives, in order to ensure that staff become and remain familiar with an operating system which is different from that which is used on a day-to-day basis, and also to understand how many essential daily procedures may be changed by the presence of this new model.

Such training is generally accompanied by considerable additional training costs for the organization involved, and it may divert carefully budgeted staff to needed training initiatives, instead of providing necessary services for the patients who are in their care. It may be argued that in most societies, hospitals and healthcare organizations operate with limited budgets, and are often faced with competing priorities, most of which provide an immediate benefit to the patient population. The potential impacts of such mandatory additional training costs should, in all cases, be carefully considered by the relevant government agency, prior to imposition on the hospitals; they may have an immediate adverse effect on carefully budgeted patient care services which the government could not have foreseen. That is not to say that such organizations do not require command and control models which are compatible, only that this mandatory "one model fits all" approach may be, at best, misguided. Compatible, interoperable, and identical are not necessarily the same things.

With all of the above being said, it may well be that some degree of mandatory standardization has validity within specific sectors of the response. There is merit in ensuring that all of the police operate in the same way, or all of the fire departments, or all of the healthcare providers. In the UK, the frameworks for response, while standardized, are developed for specific sectors. The National Health Service does provide a mandatory framework for Emergency Preparedness, Response and Resiliency for all types of healthcare providers, which meet the needs of the healthcare system, but do not follow precisely the same model as the emergency services.[8] The key to success with such an approach is to ensure that while the specific needs of both organizations and sectors are respected, the issue of creating points of integration between agencies is also addressed.

Healthcare-Specific Resources

The use of such Command-and-Control methodology is not new to healthcare, although it has not typically been specifically described as such in the past. The basic elements of a Command-and-Control model are much less "alien" to healthcare professionals than one might at first think. After all, hospitals and healthcare professionals might be argued to be in the crisis management business, and to deal with some level of crisis, albeit on a smaller scale, almost every day. This method of controlling actions and resources can actually be found in various places in the practice of modern medicine, if one simply looks closely enough. The extent to which such models have found their way into the healthcare setting is often somewhat driven by the degree of criticality of the situation being managed, and by the absolute need to eliminate errors from the activity which is occurring.

To illustrate, take a look at a typical operating theater. Everything revolves around the medical needs of a single, extremely vulnerable, patient, whose condition and safety are the paramount priorities. Now apply the basic ICS model to that setting. The lead surgeon is the Incident Commander, the assisting surgeon is the Operations Lead, the anaesthetist is the Safety Officer, the circulating nurse is the Logistics Lead, the scrub nurse is doing Short-Term Planning, the charge nurse for the OR is doing Long-Term Planning, and also some Liaison and Public Information, as required.

The principal objective is the safe resolution of the patient's medical issues, and the lead surgeon has conducted the appropriate research, and has formulated a clear and concise plan for achieving this goal, set objectives and assigned work to the individuals on the team, all the while being fully supported by the team members. The patient will even be moved to the RECOVERY Room, in order to ensure that their condition returns to normal or "near-normal," when the procedure is completed. When all goes according to plan, the patient's situation is improved, and they return to their hospital bed, better for the work that the team has accomplished, and when things occasionally go wrong, the resources are already in place and organized to address that contingency effectively.

This type of scenario is not unfamiliar to front line staff, even if they have never heard the term "Command and Control model." One can make similar arguments, differing primarily by scale, for the regular utilization of a Command-and-Control model by a trauma resuscitation team, a cardiac arrest team, or for managing the patient load in the Emergency Room or the Outpatient Department. Indeed, the model has some applicability in virtually every critical care setting in any hospital. It must always be remembered that during any crisis in a healthcare setting, front line staff, including physicians, nurses, and all other professional staff do what they always do; for them the differences in crisis response are not of scope, but of scale. It is the managers and the administration of the facility whose jobs and tasks will change, and who need to be able to do things differently.

On some levels, the roles within the Command-and-Control model of a healthcare system may be quite different from those of community agencies, even when the role labels are identical. To illustrate, in all cases, the Operations position is specialized, dealing primarily with the core business of the organization, whatever that core business might happen to be. As a single example of fundamental differences in roles, we shall compare and contrast the role of Safety Officer, within a fire department and a hospital setting.

In a fire department, the organizational role is likely to deal with fire suppression, rescue, and hazardous materials, while in a hospital, it will be about the throughput and care of patients; those generated by the emergency, and also those who were already present in the hospital when the emergency occurred. Similarly, the Safety role in a fire department is likely to be about personal protective equipment, exposure tracking and documentation, and procedural safety, but in a hospital, it may be about infection control and prevention, radiological protection, or the safe use of medical devices.

With a fire department Safety Officer, the role is likely to be primarily about personal protective equipment (for firefighters), fatigue monitoring, and oversight of decontamination procedures. In a hospital, while some of those things might take place on a limited basis, the issue of safety often deals with the impacts of medical procedures and devices, about which a fire department Safety Officer would have little or no understanding. When considered in the light of the ability of this role to stop procedures which they believe to be unsafe,[9] this lack of familiarity could actually create unsafe situations, rather than resolving them.

Finally, while in communities many of those filling Key Roles in the Incident Management Team are likely to be frontline first responders and junior grade officers, pressed into service with specific instructions, those filling the same roles in hospitals are likely to be university-educated subject matter experts in their own right, with extensive experience working in a primarily clinical environment, and who must be credentialed in order to operate inside a healthcare facility,[10] as a matter of both patient safety and hospital liability exposure. As a direct result of these realities, while there are many at various levels of governments and sectors of emergency management who advocate that such Key Role positions should be jointly operated or interchangeable between agencies, in the healthcare sector, this is simply not possible.

Hospital Incident Command System

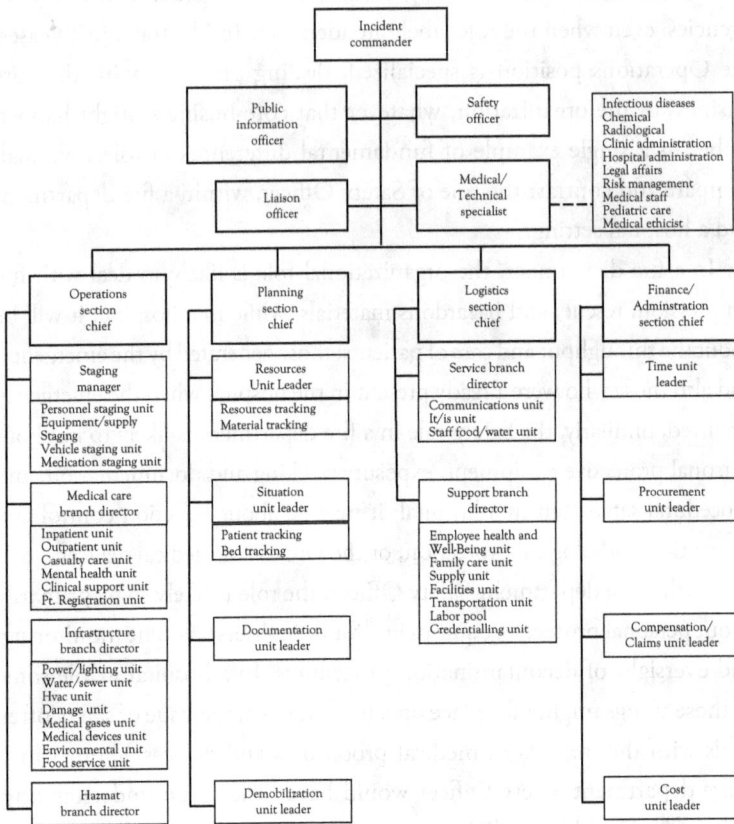

Figure 2.1 Basic Hospital Incident Command System

History

The HICS Command-and-Control model has its origins in the Hospital Emergency Incident Command System,[11] which was first introduced by the California Hospital Association in the late 1980s. The model was the first such attempt to introduce a specialized Command-and-Control model across a large sector, and the first such model in a healthcare setting. The model was felt to be necessary in order to make the then recently introduced ICS more applicable to hospitals and healthcare agencies, and to improve levels of coordination between hospitals and emergency services, which were using the ICS model. Now in its fourth version, the name has been shortened to the HICS, and its use has spread to hospitals and healthcare agencies across the United States and elsewhere. It is estimated that more than 6,000 hospitals and healthcare agencies are current users of HICS. The model is derived directly from the ICS model and can be fully integrated with it. It meets Joint Commission Accreditation Standards,[12] and is also fully National Incident Management System compliant.[13] Training in this model is available from a variety of sources, including online training programs offered by the California Hospital Association.[14]

Normal Operations

HICS, like all other ICS models, is intended to be both modular and scalable, in order to adequately address the specific needs of both the healthcare organization and the type and nature of the incident which is occurring.[15] The size and structure of the model will also be driven, to some extent, by the size of the facility and the number of resources which are available for incident response. Under normal circumstances, an Incident Commander will be identified, who will then attempt to populate all of the Command and General Staff positions, in order of perceived priority and availability. Once this has occurred, any additional positions which are required are normally backfilled, as resources become available.

In the HICS model, there is tremendous reliance upon the population of all Command and General Staff roles by individuals who have received advance training, rather than short-term population with "ad-hoc" staff, and, as a result, the activation of the model may be slowed in some circumstances. Hospitals are large, complex entities, and the Command-and-Control model during a disaster can quickly escalate in size and complexity. The challenge may be to achieve the required size without affecting patient care services, or the ability to sustain a protracted operation of the model. In order to maintain reasonable spans of control, it may be that it will be necessary to "sector" key areas of service delivery under the various areas, such as sectoring the Emergency Department or the Operating Rooms, under Operations. Such sectoring may be based upon geographic considerations (e.g., hospital "wings or multiple operating sites"), or they may be based upon type of services being provided (e.g., surgery or "critical care areas").

Special Functions

This model has been identified as a suitable Command-and-Control tool to manage hospitals not only during disaster responses but also for planned events. These could include planned utility interruptions, the planned movement of patient populations to new facilities, and labor disruptions. HICS can also be used to provide a framework for the preplanning of emergency responses.

Strengths

Because not all contingencies can be fully anticipated, particularly during a disaster, the model provides for planned improvisation in response to changing and evolving situations.[16]

The model maintains a relatively high degree of flexibility and fluidity, becoming larger or smaller as needed, and allows for the activation of only those roles that are actually required at any given time.

The model provides for an ability to maintain spans of control through the "sectoring" of service delivery, either geographically, or by service delivery sector.

The model is fully integrated and compliant with the National Incident Management System.[17] This represents an advantage to American hospitals.

Weaknesses

When fully implemented, the model can be somewhat large and cumbersome. The exceeding of recommended spans of control may occur with some regularity (see Figure 10.1).

When fully implemented, many hospitals and healthcare agencies, particularly those smaller and more isolated rural agencies, would be challenged to find sufficient resources to populate all of the roles, without affecting service delivery.

The model places less emphasis on the use of "ad-hoc" staff, instead of predesignated staff that may not be immediately available, in order to achieve truly rapid activation.

Healthcare Emergency Command-and-Control System

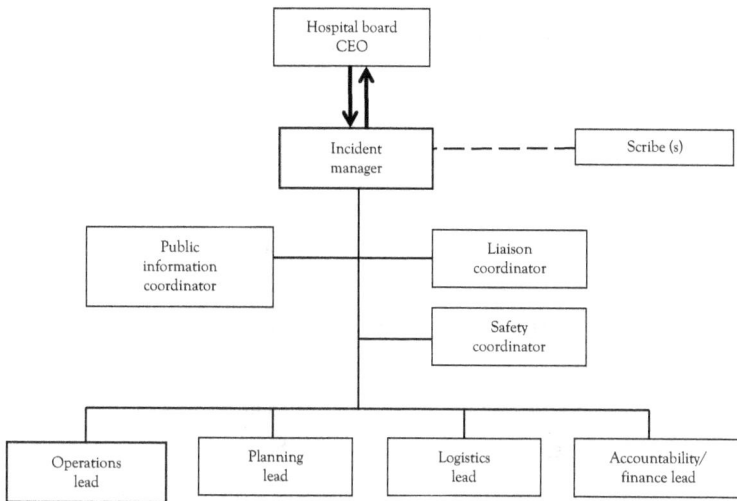

Figure 2.2 Basic Healthcare Emergency Command-and-Control System Structure

History

The HECCS model was introduced in 2011 by the Ontario (Canada) Hospital Association, for recommended use in its 200 member hospitals. The organization had been providing training in the IMS to its member facilities since 2003, but it was felt that the mainstream IMS model was strong, and remained useful, but did not fully address the specific needs of a healthcare facility during a crisis.

Chief among its concerns was the concept of the interchangeability of key role staff, as it was felt that hospitals were too specialized and had too many liability issues to permit the filling of key roles by those from other organizations who lacked familiarity with either the environment or the operating issues. Further, there was a concern that there appeared to be an expectation that trained staff from the healthcare facility might be "borrowed" by the community at a time when they were actually needed in their own environment. In the United States, a similar set of concerns had led healthcare to the development of the HICS model.

It was felt that a healthcare-specific model was required. The HICS model was examined but was found to present its own specific concerns.

The minimum staffing model generated a large enough demand for staffing that it presented potential problems for the local healthcare operating model, as it would actually require the removal of staff from patient care roles in many facilities, in order to simply staff all of the required positions. It was felt that, apart from a few large teaching facilities, this would be a problem.

It was also felt that with such a large number of participants operating in the Command-and-Control model, consultation and decision making could become cumbersome, and might actually lead to a slowing of the ability to arrive at decisions and react effectively to evolving situations during a crisis. Finally, there was a concern that all hospitals tend to be organized according to their own specific needs and experiences, and that the assignment of specific functions to specific key role positions might result in hospitals which adopted the model having to either completely re-structure their day-to-day operations, or to completely re-organize themselves to a largely unfamiliar reporting structure each time that a crisis occurred.

The model was designed with the specific requirements of hospitals and other healthcare facilities in mind, with a small, trained cadre of individuals in key role positions, enabling meetings to be short, and reactions to occur quickly, when required. It also created multiple layers of redundancy, with numerous individuals trained for each specific role. The model recognized the operational reality of hospitals, by ensuring that the model provided specific tools which permitted its activation and short-term operation by "ad-hoc" staff until the predesignated staff could arrive, outside of normal business hours.

The model also standardized the "key roles" of the upper tier of the IMS model, while recognizing that each hospital would assign responsibility and subordinate reporting to the key role staff, based upon its own individual day-to-day procedures and operating realities. The model was further strengthened by short course training, and a certification process for emergency managers wishing to work in a healthcare setting,[18] which can be delivered on-site at individual hospitals, if required, and a comprehensive tool kit for implementation.

Normal Operations

Under normal circumstances, the organization will operate under the direction of a predesignated Incident Manager, who is responsible for the analysis of events and situations and the assignment of work, and who has a direct reporting relationship with either the hospital CEO or with the Board of Trustees. All authority and responsibility for the response to whatever the emergency might happen to be is vested in the Incident Manager.

The Incident Manager may then delegate the authority (but not the responsibility) for specific, defined functions to predesignated individuals who will occupy the seven Key Roles on the organization chart (Figure 2.2). None of these positions is mandatory; they all exist at the pleasure of the Incident Manager, as and when they are actually required, and may be stood down, once they are no longer required. The Incident Manager is actually delegating elements of their own authority, in order to get work done.

The Incident Manager may, subject to guidelines, activate the Hospital Command Center, or some other appropriate Point of Command, as well as a Media Information Center, a Family Information Center, and a Staff Reporting/Staging Area, as facilities deemed to be potentially valuable to the operation of a healthcare facility, during any type of crisis. If the event is large enough that it cannot be managed with the immediately available resources, the Incident Manager is also authorized to activate any emergency staff recall procedures, such as fan-out lists. The Incident Manager may also order the activation of expanded triage/treatment spaces, or the evacuation of the facility, as required. The Incident Manager may also, in consultation with senior management, order the suspension of outpatient and other day services, and may, in consultation with the Chief of Staff, order the suspension of nonemergency surgery for the duration of the emergency.

Regular meetings of key role staff, called Business Cycle meetings, will occur in order to facilitate the exchange of information, status updates, progress reports, problems encountered, and the assignment of new tasks. The frequency and duration of the Business Cycle are flexible, based upon the needs of the incident, and are determined by the Incident Manager.

All meetings are documented, in terms of an Event Log, and are reported through regular Situation Reports during the event, and After-Action Reports following the event. The event response will stand down, once the Incident Manager, in consultation with senior management, determines that it is safe and appropriate to return the facility to normal operations, with a plan for restoration of normal services being formulated and approved in advance. The HECCS Command-and-Control model is derived directly from the mainstream IMS model, and, as a result, can operate without complication with any other organization which is using the IMS or ICS model.

Special Functions

This model has been identified as a suitable Command-and-Control tool to manage hospitals not only during disaster responses but also for planned events. These could include planned utility interruptions, the planned movement of patient populations to new facilities, and labor disruptions. HECCS can also be used to provide a framework for the preplanning of emergency responses.

The model recognizes a need for at least one full-time Scribe, in order to support the Incident Manager with the documentation of decisions and actions. While other models sometimes recognize the potential need for such a position, this is the only model which mandates its development as a permanent feature, and the predesignation of specific staff to the role.

The model also recognizes the need for a cadre of support staff to provide services for those actually operating as the HECCS Team. The presence of such staff appears to be implicit in other models, but only in the HECCS model are specific roles and requirements preidentified.

The model recognizes that only very rarely will a hospital or other healthcare facility possess a dedicated, purpose-built Command Centre from which to operate during any emergency. In most cases, the Command Center will be a multiuse space, such as a Boardroom, incorporating the use of some type of equipment "kit" for its conversion to purpose. Moreover, the development of backup operating locations, in addition to the primary location, will be required in case the emergency event denies the use of the primary designated operating location. The HECCS model recognizes this through the use of case-specific Annexes and Job Action Sheets which are expressly created to meet this need.

Strengths

The HECCS model can be activated and implemented by inexperienced staff, using written, preapproved, and easy-to-follow guidelines called Job Action Sheets, which are found in the Annexes of each copy of the Emergency Response Plan in the facility. These provide clear, unequivocal "trigger points" for activation, thereby removing any uncertainty on the part of "ad-hoc" staff. There is a clear expectation that "ad-hoc" staff will be replaced by predesignated individuals, and their previous decisions and actions confirmed, as soon as the predesignated staff member arrives. As a result, even after hours, the model can be activated quickly; often with most of the activation steps completed and the management of the incident underway, prior to the arrival of the predesignated staff.

The model allows for the assignment of multiple roles to a single individual over the short term, either for relatively small incidents, or during the early stages of large incidents when resources are not immediately available. Specific roles are preidentified for short-term "pairing," based upon a similarity of functions. To illustrate, the Public Information and Liaison functions are both primarily about the sharing of information, albeit with different groups. As a result, these two functions may be paired, over the short term, until resources become available. Similarly, the Incident Manager may simply decide to retain direct control of the Operations function, in addition to their regular duties, during a small incident, or when appropriate resources are not immediately available. Logistics is typically about various types of resources, which have monetary costs, and Finance deals with monetary costs, so short-term "pairing" of these functions may also be feasible.

The model provides specific resources which may be essential to a hospital or a healthcare facility, but largely unknown in other types of agencies. These include facilities for the triage of arriving patients, the decanting of a hospital in order to make room for new patients, the distribution or the re-distribution of disaster-related patients among multiple hospitals in order to balance workload distribution or to meet specific clinical needs. They also include the outright evacuation of the facility; a situation in which the hospital also needs to retain direct control over when, how, and to where, each patient will be evacuated, because of specific clinical requirements. Such issues are rarely considered in "mainstream" IMS and ICS models, which often have no expertise in the issues surrounding a healthcare facility, and they may not even permit "deviation" from what they regard as a "standardized" model or framework for response.

The model is sufficiently flexible to permit its application to all manner of abnormal events. This can often reduce staff training costs associated with the model, as using the model, specifically the case-specific Annexes and Job Action Sheets, for smaller emergencies such as a single missing patient, means that staff will very likely have already been exposed to the model when a large event, such as a mass-casualty incident occurs. This results in a "change in culture" for the organization, in which the HECCS model is not something unfamiliar which is introduced only during a major crisis, but rather, quickly becomes "the way that we manage every abnormal event in this hospital."

Another strength of the HECCS model is its ability to act not only as a response framework, but also as an advance planning framework for the facility. It is perfectly appropriate to break down the advance planning and procedural development associated with the Emergency Response Plan into those key issues which every organization must at least consider during a crisis. As a result, the development of Emergency Preparedness subcommittees focused on each of the seven key roles provides an appropriate planning framework. By staffing the subcommittees with those with primary and secondary responsibilities for predesignated roles, the work becomes directly relevant, and the plans and procedures are created by those who are most likely to have to implement them during a real event.

Weaknesses

The most fundamental weakness in this model is that shared with virtually every Command-and-Control model. In order to be effective, and to be remembered by staff, it must be practiced regularly. This means a need for regular training updates and exercise practice, particularly for predesignated staff. If an event occurs on a regular basis, this focus on exercises may not be required, but will remain necessary for all types of events which have not occurred, if for no other reason than as a "refresher." While the case-specific Annexes and Job Action Sheets will suffice for "ad-hoc" staff over the short term, they are intended as a stopgap measure, to be used only until such time as the designated staff arrives.

Formalizing Supporting Roles

```
Scribe(s)
Office manager
I/T Support
Telecommunications support
Dietary
Housekeeping
Security
```

Figure 2.3 HECCS supporting roles

One of the most commonly overlooked strengths of the Command-and-Control models used in the healthcare sector is the ability to tap specialized resources which are generally already operating within the facility. While the generic and mainstream models may require individuals in support roles, they will often have to source such individuals and obtain their use, or appoint individuals to provide these functions, whether or not they are a part of their day-to-day duties, on an "ad-hoc" basis. In doing so, it may be necessary to take these individuals away from other needed functions. To illustrate, during a crisis, is a uniformed policeman more valuable on the street, or providing security at the entrance to the municipal Emergency Operations Center?

Fortunately, in the healthcare setting, there is a need for such resources on a daily basis. Almost all hospitals already have security guards, housekeeping staff, engineering staff, dietary staff, clerical staff, and so on. Indeed, it can be argued that, with the possible exception of the smallest hospitals, every type of service which is available in the community at large has an analog operating inside the hospital, albeit on a smaller scale.

Knowing that such individuals are available on a continual basis within the hospital allows the Emergency Manager to secure the services of these individuals in advance, and actually formally incorporate their roles into both the Command-and-Control model and the Emergency Plan itself.

Choosing a Model

While compliance with legislated mandates and standards is both necessary and desirable, the choice of Command-and-Control model should, in the opinion of the author, remain the prerogative of each healthcare agency. The first priority of any Command-and-Control model should be the effective response of the organization to whatever crisis or disaster is occurring. Organizations, when left to their own devices, typically choose a model which best meets the specific needs and realities of their own organization and its core business. In many cases, imposed Command-and-Control models tend to improve interagency coordination at the direct expense of meeting, or in some cases, even recognizing those needs, within each participating organization. In those circumstances in which the Emergency Manager has the latitude to do so, any choice of a Command-and-Control model for a hospital or a healthcare agency should be made with a priority placed on meeting the specific needs of the organization, with interagency coordination being viewed as a highly desirable secondary consideration.

Interoperability

	ICS	IMS	HICS	HECCS	USNIMS	UKIMS
Policy	Elected local authority	Elected local authority	Ceo/hospital board	Ceo/Hospital board	Elected local/state/ federal authority	Platinum (Cobra)
Strategy	Incident commander	Incident manager	Incident commander	Incident manager	Incident commander	Gold
Tactical	Command and general staff groups	Command and general staff groups	Command and general staff groups	Command and general staff groups	Command and general staff groups	Silver
Task	Group leaders	Frontline staff	Unit leaders/ directors	Frontline staff	Response resources	Bronze

Figure 2.4 Command-and-Control system interoperability

Despite the differences of many of the Command-and-Control systems, both specialized and generic, which are in current use, integration and interoperability is both feasible and relatively easy to accomplish. Despite the differences in titles, the fundamental reporting relationships, and, in most cases, the basic labels of each model are relatively identical (see Figure 2.4). Safety remains Safety, Planning remains Planning, and so on. Typically, effective coordination of the resources of multiple agencies may be achieved using one of four approaches.

The first approach to coordination is the co-location or conferencing of those at the Strategy level (Incident Commanders, Incident Managers, Incident Controllers, and Gold Command). This is the normal method of major incident coordination in the British Gold, Silver, Bronze model. It is also not uncommon among the command officers of the various emergency services while operating at the site of a major incident. In the case of emergency services, they may elect to choose a single commander, they may agree to a joint command operation, or they may transfer command among themselves, based upon the specific major expertise and resource requirements of each discreet stage of the incident response.

The second approach to coordination is the creation of interagency Task Forces, as is practiced in both the generic ICS and the U.S. National Incident Management System models. In such cases, the Task level resources of two or more agencies may be placed under the authority of a single individual, and they may be assigned to perform specific functions. A Heavy Urban Search and Rescue team is an excellent example of such a resource, with police officers providing security and searching for survivors, firefighters providing access and extrication for victims, heavy equipment operators supporting firefighters in the rescue function, and paramedics providing medical care to victims both during and following extrication. Most examples of such Task Forces, however, occur on an "ad-hoc" basis, and are usually intended and tailored to meet the specific needs of each incident.

In the third approach, the local authority, usually an elected Council, will name a specific individual, often the Fire Chief or the Police Chief, to lead the emergency response resources through any major crisis or incident response. This is most common in small communities in which all of the response resources belong to that actual community and are not going to be operated by other levels of government or private providers. This model is most effective when the arrangements are agreed upon well in advance, and the participating agencies have the opportunity to train and work together, and when they have developed a "trust" of one another.

One of the challenges is that, not unlike some of the Command-and-Control models already discussed, the appointment of a single individual from one particular agency may mean that the person in charge does not have a truly comprehensive understanding of the knowledge, skills, resources, or capabilities of all of the agencies which he or she is supervising. With the advent of more formal Command-and-Control models, this particular approach to multiagency coordination is slowly disappearing from common usage.

The fourth approach utilizes the elements of the Tactical level of the various Command-and-Control models. It takes the position that those at the Strategy level are essentially too busy appropriately evaluating information and assessing and directing their own response to become a point of coordination. As a result, those at the Tactical level become highly effective points of coordination across multiple agencies. This occurs through each of the actual role labels, with Logistics teaming with Logistics from other agencies, Public Information doing the same, and so on.

The result is very similar to the Task Forces employed in both the generic ICS model, and in the US National Incident Management System model. The important difference is that in this approach, the Task Forces will be role-specific, instead of task-specific. In this manner, it is entirely possible for independent Logistics operations from each agency to support one another, for all of the Public Information people from the various agencies to come together and formulate a single, comprehensive media plan and consistent associated messaging, and so on. Such an approach, while highly effective and highly desirable, requires both training and regular practice.

Student Projects

Student Project #1

Examine the HICS Command-and-Control model in detail. Select a single, simple, disaster scenario, and describe how the hospital under study would have its response efforts integrated with those of the emergency services located in the community served by the hospital, using the National Incident Management System. Identify three strengths to this approach, and also three weaknesses to the approach, proposing solutions for the weaknesses identified. Construct a logical argument either for or against this approach to integration, defending your positions appropriately. Ensure that all information is suitably and appropriately cited and referenced, in order to demonstrate that the appropriate research has occurred.

Student Project #2

Examine the HECCS Command-and-Control model in detail. Select a single, simple, disaster scenario, and describe how the hospital under study would have its response efforts integrated with those of the emergency services located in the community served by the hospital, using the National Incident Management System. Identify three strengths to this approach, and also three weaknesses to the approach, proposing solutions for the weaknesses identified. Construct a logical argument either for or against this approach to integration, defending your positions appropriately. Ensure that all information is suitably and appropriately cited and referenced, in order to demonstrate that the appropriate research has occurred.

Test Your Knowledge

Take your time. Read each question carefully and select the MOST CORRECT answer for each. The correct answers appear at the end of the section. If you score less than 80 percent (eight correct answers), you should re-read this chapter.

1. Specialized Command-and-Control models may be required in a healthcare setting because mainstream models often:

   (a) Fail to address important clinical realities
   (b) Use interchangeable staff in Key Roles

(c) Can impose additional training costs

(d) All of the above

2. The HICS has its origins in the:

(a) Gold, Silver, Bronze System

(b) Incident Command System

(c) U.S. National Incident Management System

(d) Australian AIIMS System

3. In the Healthcare Emergency Command-and-Control System, those roles which are immediately subordinate to the Incident Manager are called:

(a) Command Staff

(b) General Staff

(c) Key Roles

(d) Supporting Roles

4. In generic Command-and-Control models, it may be possible to use trained staff interchangeably between organizations. This practice is impossible in healthcare settings, because:

(a) Healthcare settings are too specialized

(b) It is illegal to do so

(c) Healthcare staff are more difficult to manage

(d) The roles are completely different

5. One of the most significant strengths of the HECCS model, is:

(a) Everyone in healthcare already understands it

(b) The ability to use ad-hoc staff to activate the model over the short term

(c) The ability to communicate quickly with the hospital's trustees

(d) All of the above

6. In the United States, any healthcare based Command-and-Control model is required by law to be:

(a) Compliant with accreditation standards
(b) Compliant with international standards
(c) Compliant with the U.S. National Incident Management System model
(d) All of the above

7. One of the greatest challenges with complete interagency standardization to a single Command-and-Control models is that such practices typically achieve standardization at the expense of:

(a) Agency-specific needs
(b) Agency-specific preferences
(c) Previous training
(d) Both (a) and (b)

8. Healthcare-specific Command-and-Control models are able to fully integrate with most other Command-and-Control models by creating formal points of coordination at the:

(a) Strategy level
(b) Tactical level
(c) Task level
(d) Policy level

9. A significant strength of both of the healthcare Command-and-Control models discussed, is that in addition to managing disaster/crisis response, it is also possible to use them for:

(a) Managing scheduled events
(b) Managing special events
(c) Creating a planning framework
(d) All of the above

10. By linking together similar positions across the Command-and-Control models of all agencies responding to a disaster/crisis, it becomes possible to:

(a) Create role-specific Task Forces
(b) Provide joint work direction
(c) Source unusual items
(d) All of the above

Answers

1. (d)   2. (b)   3. (c)   4. (a)   5. (b)
6. (c)   7. (a)   8. (b)   9. (d)   10. (a)

Additional Reading

The author recommends the following exceptionally good titles as supplemental readings, which will help to enhance the student's knowledge of those topics covered in this chapter:

CHA. 2014. ICS/NIMS Online Training Course, California Hospital Association website, www.calhospitalprepare.org/icsnims-online-course (accessed February 25, 2014).

ICS Canada. 2012. Incident Command System Operational Description, ICS Canada, .pdf document, www.icscanada.ca/images/upload/ICS%20OPS%20Description2012.pdf (accessed February 28, 2014).

IS-100.HCB: Introduction to the Incident Command System (ICS 100) for Healthcare/Hospitals, Independent Study Course, http://training.fema.gov/EMIWeb/IS/courseOverview.aspx?code=IS-100.HCb (accessed March 01, 2014).

National Health Service. 2013. Core Standards for Emergency Preparedness, Response and Resiliency, NHS Commissioning Board, London, www.england.nhs.uk/wp-content/uploads/2013/03/eprr-core-standards.pdf (accessed February 28, 2014).

OHA. 2009. Emergency Management Toolkit: Developing a Sustainable Emergency Management Program for Hospitals, Ontario Hospital Association, Toronto.

CHAPTER 3

Key Roles in Command-and-Control for Healthcare

Introduction

No Command-and-Control model can function without people. The organization table and the reporting structures only work effectively when they are occupied. Hospitals and healthcare agencies are somewhat unique, in that many, or indeed, most, already possess residential expertise in most of the areas of knowledge and skill sets which are required to guide the facility through any incident. It is often a matter of identifying that expertise and pressing it into service.

This chapter will examine those roles which are the specific requirements of a healthcare-based Command-and-Control model. The duties, the reporting structures, and the potential subordinate staffing arrangements for each will be examined in detail, along with methods of using these roles as highly effective points of coordination/collaboration between the healthcare organization and outside agencies, including those in the community. In each case, we will attempt to identify suitable candidates in terms of both knowledge and expertise, for each role, from within the staff pool which is normally found in most hospitals. We will also examine the short-term usage of "ad-hoc" staff in each position, along with the requirements for doing so.

This chapter will also examine the supporting staff requirements which may be anticipated. These include roles which are central to the success of the Command-and-Control model, such as the Scribe. It will also examine those support services which are required in order to permit the Incident Management Team to function in an environment which is conducive to success, and which is as seamless as it is possible to make it. In each case, we will attempt to identify the potential sources of such personnel, and how to obtain their use. It should also be noted that, while work areas are organized under specific Key Roles in this chapter, these are merely suggestions. Every hospital and healthcare facility already has an organizational reporting structure, which is based upon local need and local realities. The intent here is to standardize the Strategy and Tactical levels; the Task level remains, organizationally, a matter of local autonomy. None of the subordinates listed are mandatory, they are simply suggestions.

Learning Objectives

Upon completion of this chapter, the student should be able to clearly describe each of the Key Roles for a healthcare-based Command-and-Control system, along with their responsibilities, appropriate selection criteria, and reporting relationships. The student should also be able to describe appropriate supporting positions for each of the Key Roles, as well as those positions which, while not an official feature of the Command-and-Control model, are nevertheless essential to its success. Finally, the student will be able to describe those support resources which are required in order to make the functioning of the Incident Management Team as smooth and "seamless" as possible.

Incident Manager

Every incident is best resolved when a single person assumes both responsibility and control of the response efforts. The title of this individual will vary, according to the Command-and-Control model which is in use, but the role and duties remain essentially unchanged. They may be known as the Incident Commander (USNIMS,[1] Incident Command System [ICS], Hospital Incident Command System [HICS]), the Incident Manager (Incident Management System,[2] Healthcare Emergency Command and Control System [HECCS]), the Incident Controller (Australasian Inter-Service Incident Management System[3]), or the Gold Commander (UKNIMS). Regardless of the title, this is the leadership role for all Command-and-Control models and is the organization's principal strategist for the response to the event.

The Incident Manager holds both the authority and the responsibility for the resolution of the incident. While authority for a given portfolio of duties may be delegated to a subordinate, the responsibility always remains with the Incident Manager. The Incident Manager is responsible for determining which of the other Incident Management Team Key Roles are required, and for the appointment of individuals to fill these roles. All of the Key Roles exist in order to lighten the burden of the Incident Manager through the delegation of workload, in order to permit the Incident Manager to focus more exclusively on the actual high-level management of the incident. No role, other than the Incident Manager, is automatically created; all roles exist as and when the Incident Manager determines that they are required and may be terminated when the Incident Manager decides that they are no longer needed.

The Incident Manager is responsible for the creation of a formal or improvised Incident Action Plan,[4] the setting of goals and objectives and their assignment as individual tasks and duties, and for monitoring these for both progress and completion. The purpose of such a plan is to guide the organization through the crisis, to its successful resolution. The Incident Manager is, in essence, a Project Manager, and the Incident Action Plan may be quite correctly viewed as a formal Project Plan. If created correctly, it will include essential and nonessential but desirable tasks, an order of completion, milestones, and timelines for completion, complete with a critical path. As a result, good project management training and the associated skills are highly desirable in an Incident Manager.

The Incident Manager will conduct an initial briefing for all Key Role staff and will set a schedule for the group's Business Cycle meetings. The timing and duration of such meetings will be periodically adjusted by the Incident Manager, in order to meet the needs of the organization and the demands of the incident. The Incident Manager will also meet with those at the Policy level of the organization, in order to ensure that they are adequately briefed regarding the nature of the incident and its impacts on the organization. The Incident Manager is also responsible for all of the documentation associated with the incident, including the Incident

Log, the Incident Action Plan,[5] Situation Reports (Sitreps),[6] Post-Event Debriefing Reports, and After-Action Reports.[7]

Those filling the role of Incident Manager should be predesignated within any healthcare organization. There should always be a number of predesignated individuals which is sufficient to provide the depth to rotate on-call assignments and to facilitate both 24-hour scheduling and protracted operations. Suitable candidates are those with exceptional leadership and project planning skills, a detailed knowledge of the organization and how it functions, and sufficient position authority to direct work effectively. This may be viewed as a developmental opportunity for those seeking greater responsibilities within the organization.

That being said, the operational realities of most healthcare organizations are such that almost anyone in a healthcare setting may be called upon at some point to become an "ad-hoc" Incident Manager; in small events, such as a single missing patient, it will probably fall to the Charge Nurse of the affected Unit by default. It is also possible, particularly outside of normal business hours, that an "ad-hoc" Incident Manager may need to establish control of an event, and to direct the response until such time as a designated Incident Manager can arrive to relieve them. In such cases, the organization will benefit from a clear, concise, well-written Emergency Response Plan, along with additional tools, such as Job Action Sheets, intended to support the activities and the decisions of "ad-hoc" staff until such time as the predesignated staff arrives.

The Command Group

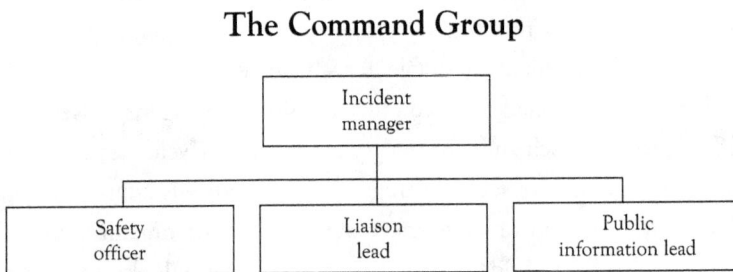

Figure 3.1 The Command Group—Basic structure

The subgroup of the Incident Management Team Key Roles, sometimes referred to as the Command Group, reports directly to the

Incident Manager. It consists of three roles which are specifically intended to lighten the workload of the Incident Manager, by the delegation of specific tasks to individuals and teams who are, for the most part, specialists. Each of these fulfills a role which is either a legislated mandate, a potential liability exposure, or an otherwise legitimate expectation of the person in charge. Each of these roles is a feature of almost every widely used Command-and-Control model. There are three such roles, the Safety Officer, the Public Information Lead, and the Liaison Lead. Each of these will be examined and discussed individually, in the context of use in a hospital/healthcare organization.

Safety Officer

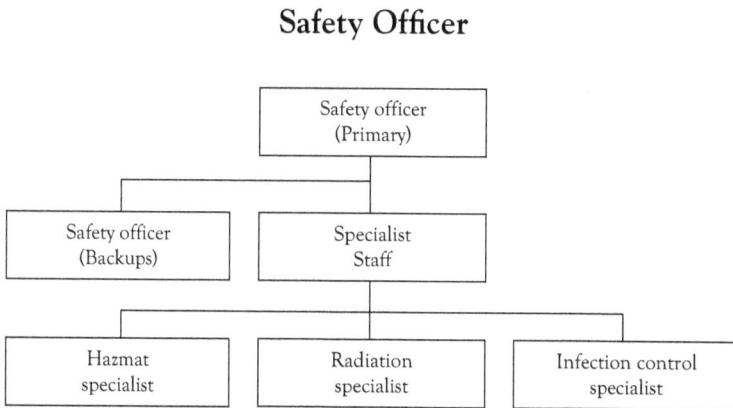

Figure 3.2 The Safety Officer Group with subordinates

The role of the Safety Officer in a hospital/healthcare setting is to take whatever measures are possible to ensure the personal safety of all of those who may be present within the facility. This includes patients, visitors, staff members, contractors, and anyone else who happens to be physically present in the facility while the incident is ongoing. This position is responsible for the ongoing monitoring of activities, work and other procedures taking place in the facility, in order to ensure safety. In most systems, the Safety Officer will be vested with the authority to order the immediate stoppage of any work or activity which they believe to be unsafe for the participants, or to represent an immediate threat to the safety of others.[8] The Safety Officer is also responsible for the ongoing review of procedures and equipment, in order to identify any potential issues related to safety. The provision of recommendations to the Incident Manager regarding changes to emergency or routine procedures and protective devices, including personal protective equipment are also within the purview of this role.

In many jurisdictions, the Incident Manager, as the "most responsible person" would be directly liable for the safety of others. Clearly, during an incident, the typical Incident Manager has too many other immediate and pressing responsibilities to devote the time and attention to the issue of safety which it deserves. As a result, they delegate this responsibility downward, preferably to a predesignated individual who possesses an appropriate background, training, and knowledge base, to provide the issue of safety with the attention which it deserves. While the use of predesignated staff is ideal, and should be used wherever possible, the operational realities of a hospital are such that the position may need to be filled over the short term, particularly outside of normal business hours, through the use of "ad-hoc" staff. With this in mind, such individuals should be supported, through the use of clear, concise, advance directions, including both the Emergency Response Plan, case-specific Annexes, and Job Action Sheets, to ensure that they can function appropriately in the position, until relieved by predesignated staff.

Selection

The role of Safety Officer is often predesignated; usually to one who fulfills a similar role on a daily basis. As an alternative, or to create depth within the position, it may also be possible to predesignate members of the organization's health and safety committee, preferably those with the longest service and highest level of training. In some jurisdictions, governments have created certification processes which ensure the competence of committee members, and such certified members are an ideal resource to expand the depth of the Safety Officer position. This role is also unique, in that the position of Safety Officer may also be staffed on the basis of specific areas of expertise, which may be determined by the nature of the actual incident.[9] To illustrate, it may be appropriate to use a Radiologist or even a technician as Safety Officer in the case of a radiation spill, or a Chemist from the hospital laboratory, in the event of a hazardous materials spill.

Interagency Integration

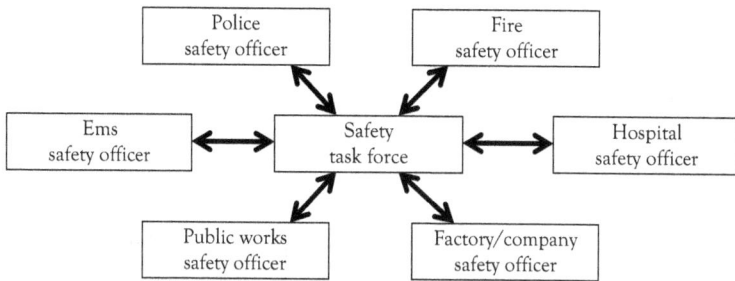

Figure 3.3 The interagency safety task force (one example)

Within the emergency services, it is not uncommon for the role of safety to fall to an inter-agency team. In the ICS, this is called a "Task Force." Essentially, each of the agency Safety Officers bring their own subject matter expertise and knowledge to the team, and they operate as a functional unit. Once the Safety vests or tabards are in place, the color of the uniform under it becomes irrelevant; any Safety Officer will review any work occurring on the site, and order the work stopped, if they believe it to be unsafe. If an interagency dispute occurs, the Safety Officer from the appropriate agency will be summoned and will issue a final ruling.

Public Information Lead

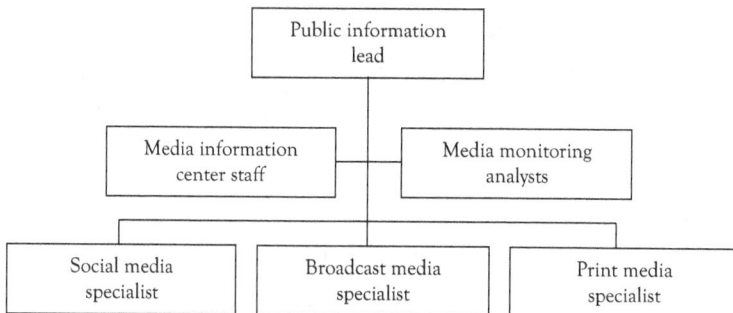

Figure 3.4 The Public Information Lead Group with subordinates

During almost any major incident, the presence of members of the media poses a significant challenge. Managed correctly, the media can be a useful tool for the Incident Management Team. Handled incorrectly, or not handled at all, their presence and activities may pose a serious problem. The first thing to remember is that the members of the media are simply doing a job; they are attempting to inform the public issues and events which they believe will be of interest. How they accomplish this is largely up to the organization, and the presence of someone with experience at dealing with the media can make an incredible difference. This is the role of the Public Information Lead.[10]

The Public Information Lead is responsible for the creation of a formal Media Plan, which operates as an Annex of the Emergency Response Plan and the Incident Action Plan. The role of such a plan is to attempt to manage the presence of the media on hospital premises, and to ensure that the correct messaging goes out to the media, and from there, to the general public. They are also responsible for the protection of confidential patient information, and for ensuring that each patient's right to privacy is not violated during their treatment in the facility. The Public Information Lead should be responsible for the operation of the hospital's Media Information Center, with the support of a number of subordinate staff. They will also be responsible for the creation of Media Releases (with prior approval of the Incident Manager), arranging media conferences, interviews, and, where appropriate, tours and photo opportunities.

The Public Information Lead is also responsible for the advance creation of supporting information for the media, such as background information handouts, and biographies of key players. This information (often called "boiler plate" by the media) should be created and approved in advance, for immediate release when necessary. In summary, the job of the Public Information Lead is to ensure that the members of the media receive information, which is accurate, appropriate, and consistent, and to ensure that the message being received is the correct one.

Selection

Almost every hospital or healthcare agency has either an individual on staff or retains the services of a consultant, who is responsible for dealing with the media on a daily basis. During a crisis, those which do not have such a person are likely to quickly discover that one is required. This individual is the logical person to perform this role during any crisis. In some cases, particularly with smaller hospitals which lack media staff, it may be necessary to negotiate a shared service arrangement between the hospital which has such a resource, and those who might require it occasionally. In either case, the candidate selected should be consulted regarding both the assignment of supporting staff and resource requirements, and those requirements should be incorporated into the Emergency Response Plan.

Interagency Integration

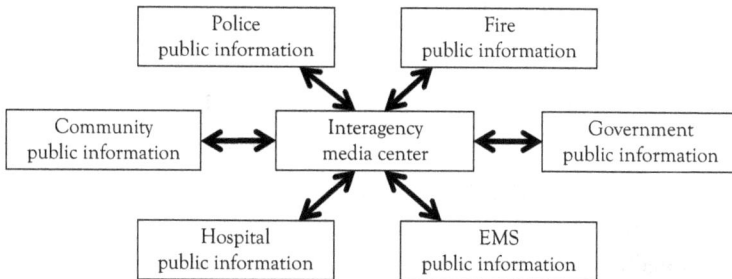

Figure 3.5 Interagency public information task force (one example)

When a group of agencies are employing similar command and control systems, it is likely that each agency will have its own Public Information Lead, or someone with a similar title and responsibilities. Each of these individuals will have access to their own sources of information, often directly relevant to their own agency's operations, and their own goals and objectives regarding the information which is to be released. That being said, there is little valid reason why the Public Information Leads from all agencies involved should not collaborate in a joint media operation, such as what might be described as a Public Information Task Force, in the ICS model. All of the Public Information Leads from all of the agencies have a closed meeting, come to an agreement, and from that point forward, a single, consistent set of information and messaging is provided to the media and the public, regardless of which source it is coming from. Agencies may deal with specific items individually, but the overall messaging remains consistent.

Liaison Lead

Figure 3.6 The Liaison Lead Group with subordinates

Every major incident is generally managed as a series of meetings. Some of these meetings are internal, such as the Business Cycle meetings, while others involve the interagency sharing of current information, problems encountered, and status. That being said, if the Incident Manager were to personally attend every meeting related to an incident, they would be left with little time in which to actually manage that incident! As a result, an ambassador of sorts is required. The role of the Liaison Lead is information sharing; in this case, to share with other responding agencies and levels of government,[11] as opposed to with the media and the general public. The role of the Liaison Lead is to attend all external meetings and telephone/video conferences on behalf of the Incident Manager, in order to share their own information with outside agencies, and to collect appropriate information from those agencies to bring back to the Incident Manager. They will, in effect, become the "face" of the hospital or healthcare agency, to the balance of the response agencies.

The "currency" of disaster management is information. Every Incident Manager requires the best possible information upon which to base the required decisions for the management of whatever crisis happens to be occurring. It is for this reason that in most Command-and-Control models, the position of Incident Manager is in fact a "nexus" of sorts for the flow of information. That being said, the flow of information can, at times, become incredibly high, and not all of it is actually required by the Incident Manager. For this reason, the Liaison Lead must function as not only an information conduit but also as a filter; allowing through the relevant information and editing the "minutia," so that the Incident Manager does not become overwhelmed by an unfiltered flow of unnecessary information.

Selection

The individuals chosen for the Liaison Lead role must be both diplomats and skilled communicators. They must also be sufficiently senior to ensure that other agencies do not perceive that they have been left to deal with a "minor functionary." A relatively senior member of the hospital's management team is often a good choice for this role. The Emergency Manager may be another good option; after all, it is rare that the Emergency Manager will be expected to actually run the incident.

Discretion is also essential; knowing how to ignore the sometimes "intense" atmosphere which occurs when individuals are under stress, and also knowing how to determine which elements of their own information should be released, and which should not. The Liaison Lead must also be a good judge of information and also reliable and trusted editor; ideally, someone who can be trusted to listen to the entire content of a 30-minute meeting, pull out the two major issues which are relevant, and return only those two issues to the Incident Manager. While one individual may be in charge of this function, it may also be possible to identify individuals who have extensive regular dealings with outside agencies and are known to them and trusted. There is no valid reason not to exploit such prior relationships; assuming that the individuals involved can be spared from their normal duties, and that such activities are centrally coordinated. It should be anticipated that this role may need to be filled over the short term by "ad-hoc" staff, until such time as predesignated staff can arrive. This reality should be supported by appropriate provisions in the Emergency Response Plan and the presence of appropriate Job Action Sheets.

Interagency Coordination

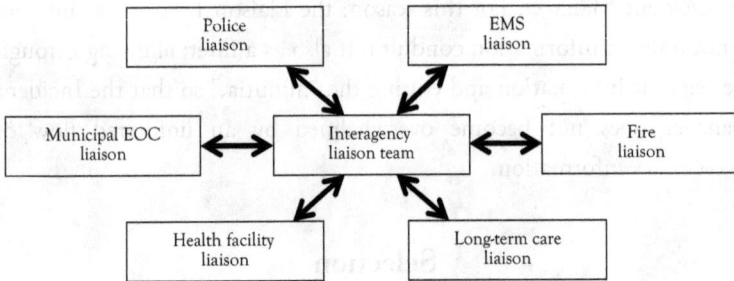

Figure 3.7 The interagency liaison task force (one example)

As has already been stated, the Incident Managers are almost never in a position to attend such meetings, due to conflicting demands on their time. The one exception to this is the UKNIMS model, in which the vast majority of information sharing, and coordination occurs through the Gold Commanders. There is no valid reason why the Liaison Leads from all agencies involved in the incident response should not schedule regular meetings, either face to face or as teleconferences, in order to provide a regular, consistent program of information sharing, so that each agency is operating based upon the best possible information from all available sources. Such meetings may be scheduled around the Business Cycle meetings of the various agencies, usually following such meetings, in order to ensure that the information being shared is absolutely current.

The General Staff

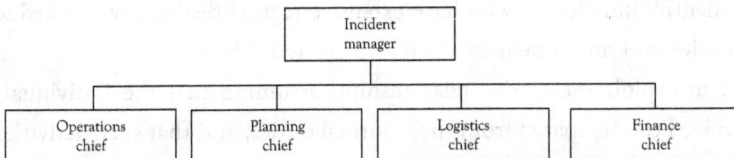

Figure 3.8 The General Staff

The General Staff group reports directly to the Incident Manager. Its function is to conduct the actual response to the incident, as well as the "core businesses" of the organization, whatever that "core business" happens to be. In the case of a hospital or a healthcare agency, this group is involved in ensuring the operation of the throughput and care of patients, and the provision of patient care-related services. The dominant role in this group is the Operations Chief, who is primarily tasked with the conduct of core business; all other roles are intended to primarily support that role, or to respond to its activities. This group, along with the Command Staff, is considered a part of the "Tactical" level in most Command-and-Control models. All of these groups have a dynamic working relationship with one another, and their collaboration is directed at supporting Operations through the process of resolving the incident. In the simplest terms, this group may be characterized as the "thinkers" (Planning), the "do-ers" (Operations), the "finders" (Logistics), and the "payers" (Finance).

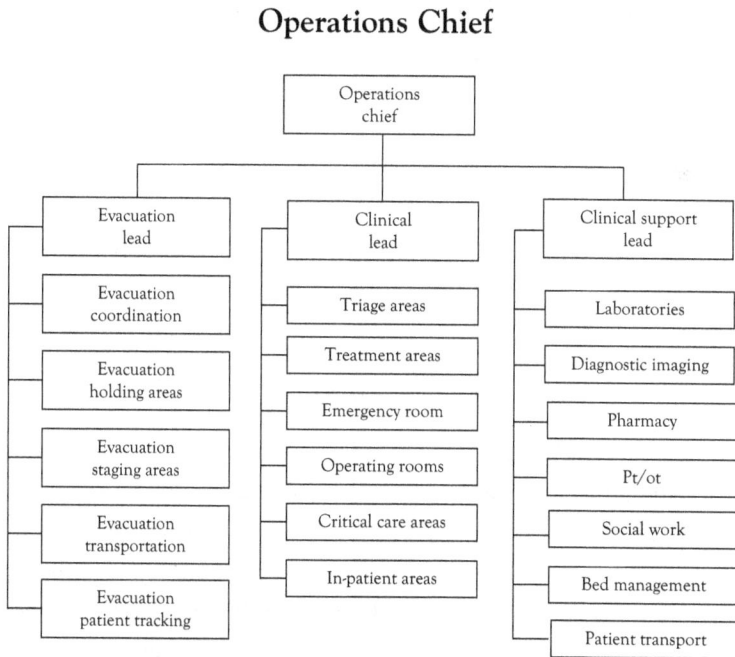

Operations Chief

Figure 3.9 The Operations Chief with subordinate roles

Operations is the second most important role in the most Command-and-Control models. The Operations Chief is the individual who is responsible for the core business of the organization, whatever that core business happens to be. In the case of a hospital or a healthcare organization, the Operations Chief is responsible for the throughput and care of all patients, whether generated by the incident being responded to, or already in the facility when the incident occurred.[12] The position is also responsible for the physical egress and removal of patients, during any evacuation scenario. This role will be instrumental in all decisions regarding patient care-related resources, including the suspension or termination of regular services, such as outpatient clinics or elective surgery. The role reports directly to the Incident Manager. All other roles in the General Staff group primarily support this position.

This role will also be responsible for the activation and operation of incident-specific treatment facilities, including triage areas, emergency treatment areas, patient holding areas, and so on. In addition to all of this, they will also ensure that all pre-existing in-patients continue to receive the care, treatment, and other services which they require. The Operations Chief's subordinates include all of those groups and services which are primarily responsible for the provision of clinical care (physician group, nursing group, operating theaters, etc.) as well as a separate line of authority which covers clinical support services (diagnostic imaging, laboratories, blood bank, medical records, etc.). In summary, this role is responsible for the provision of all services which make a hospital a hospital.

Selection

The candidates for this position should possess, above all, a strong clinical background. They should have significant experience in the hospital, and exceptional leadership skills. They must possess detailed knowledge of the facility, the services and resources available, and how things work within the facility. The most logical candidates would be very senior members of the nursing administration or the physician staff, although in many hospitals, physicians are contractors, as opposed to actual employees, and may be reluctant to accept such a role. The candidates for this role should be predesignated, with both a primary candidate and sufficient backups to ensure adequate depth of coverage for around the clock or protracted operations. It should also be recognized that this role may need to be filled over the short term by "ad-hoc" staff, probably a more senior staff nurse, until such time as the predesignated Operations Chief arrives at the facility. As a result, adequate supports will need to be present in the Emergency Response Plan, such as clear, concise, case-specific instructions for various types of events in the Annexes, and suitable Job Action Sheets.

Interagency Cooperation

This position, like that of Incident Manager, is likely to be far too busy, and is far too specialized, to provide much opportunity for interagency cooperation.

Planning Chief

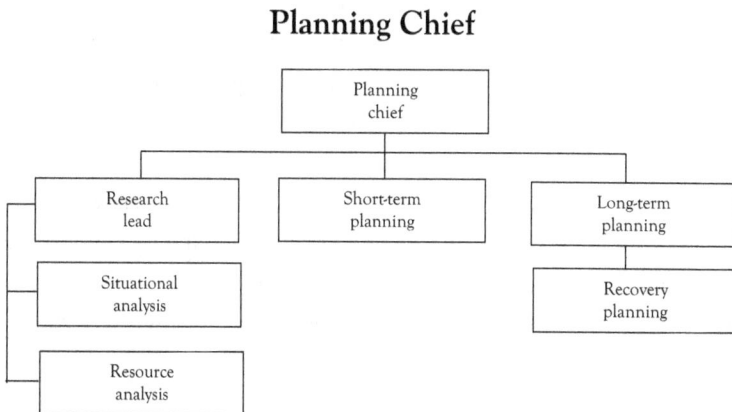

Figure 3.10 The Planning Chief with subordinate roles

The "conceptual thinker" of the organization. This individual is responsible for research, situational and resource analysis, and the identification and recommendation of both short-term (<eight hours) and long-term (eight hours+) strategies and actual plans.[13] The duties are many and varied; they might include everything from the identification of the characteristics of the chemical that is leaking from a tanker outside the hospital, to critical care bed availability in other hospitals across the region. The Planning Chief is also normally responsible for the development of a Recovery Plan,[14] which will provide for the planned and systematic transition from "disaster" mode back to normal operations. They are also generally responsible for assisting the Incident Manager in the creation

and maintenance of a formal Incident Action Plan. Subordinates typically include those with responsibility for short-term planning, long-term planning, research, situational analysis, and resource analysis. In normal circumstances, the long-term planning role eventually transitions into the recovery planning role.

Selection

The candidates for this position should possess exceptional research and project management skills. The ability to apply analytical techniques, such as Root Cause Analysis[15] and Value-Stream Mapping[16] are also useful skills, as are familiarity and comfort with research tools, such as Internet search engines, Medline, hazardous materials databases, and so on. The candidates for this role should be predesignated, with both a primary candidate and sufficient backups to ensure adequate depth of coverage for around the clock or protracted operations. In many cases, the primary position may fall to the organization's Emergency Manager. It should also be recognized that this role may need to be filled over the short term by "ad-hoc" staff, until such time as the predesignated Planning Chief arrives at the facility. As a result, adequate supports will need to be present in the Emergency Response Plan, such as clear, concise, case-specific instructions for various types of events in the Annexes, and suitable Job Action Sheets.

Interagency Cooperation

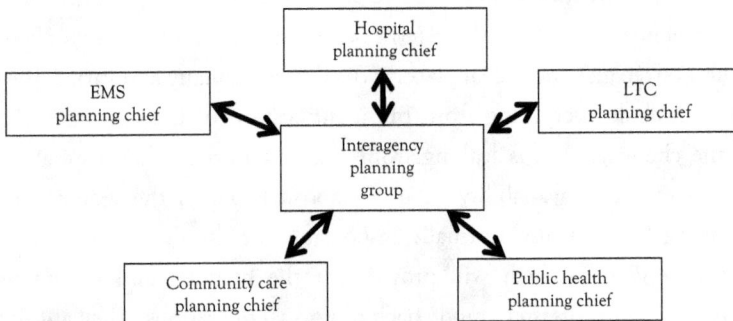

Figure 3.11 The interagency planning task force (one example)

The "currency" of disaster management and response is information, and the Planning Chiefs of each organization are its "information miners." Since any Incident Manager requires access to the best information possible in order to make decisions, it is only logical that the Planning Chiefs of all participating organizations should meet on a regular basis, either in person or by teleconference, as a Planning Task Force. This will ensure the exchange of information from all sources and can facilitate the more detailed coordination of actual plans between the agencies.

Logistics Chief

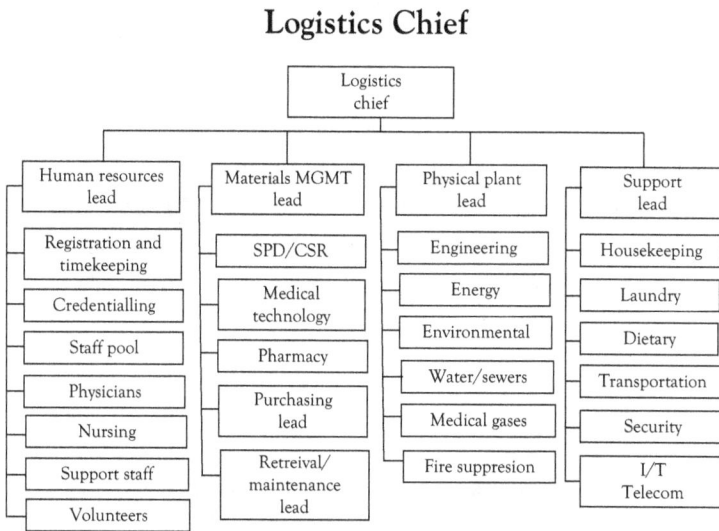

Figure 3.12 The Logistics Chief with subordinate roles

The Logistics role is primarily about providing those resources which are required in order to successfully manage the incident in question.[17] Some of those resources are material, and others are people. In many cases, the identification of specific needs may actually be collaborative, with either Operations making a specific request or Planning identifying a specific resource shortfall. Logistics deals with the sourcing, acquisition, processing, delivery, and recovery of those resources, in support of incident operations. In most hospitals and healthcare facilities, it is normally a joint operation by Materials Management and Human Resources, either jointly or with one group, normally Materials Management, assuming the leadership role.

Many healthcare facilities also organize responsibility for physical plant operations and normal support services, including security, housekeeping, dietary, and transportation under this group. This arrangement can be particularly useful in a hospital, with the potential for the creation of task-specific multigroup Task Forces, such as for the discharge of patients and the reprocessing of those beds in order to make them available to new victims who require them. To illustrate, a team consisting of the Charge Nurse, a physician, and a Discharge Planner evaluate a patient and determine that they may receive either a discharge or a transfer to an alternate venue of care. The physician writes the discharge orders. The actual discharge, along with required support services and transportation, is arranged by the Discharge Planner. Patient Transportation moves the patient to a designated Holding Area within the hospital to await transport. As the patient leaves the bed, Housekeeping cleans the room and the bed, and adds new bedding. All equipment and inventory in the room is re-stocked and a safety inspection occurs. Admitting is notified that the bed is available for the next patient who requires it, and the bed reprocessing Task Force moves on to clear and reprocess the next available bed.

Selection

The appropriate candidates for this position will have a detailed knowledge of the hospital and of how it works. They will also have an extensive knowledge of hospital purchasing procedures and supply chains for all types of resources. They will also require extensive knowledge of human resources practices and procedures. While either Materials Management or Human Resources may be able to perform this role, it is likely that the "lion's share" of the work will fall within the Materials Management sphere of influence. That being said, there is no reason why the primary should not be from Materials Management, with at least one designated backup from Human Resources. Each will need to learn the basics of the other's field, in any case. The candidates for this role should be predesignated, with both a primary candidate and sufficient backups to ensure adequate depth of coverage for around the clock or protracted operations. It should also be recognized that this role may need to be filled over the short term by "ad-hoc" staff, until such time as the predesignated Logistics Chief arrives at the facility. As a result, adequate supports will need to be present in the Emergency Response Plan, such as clear, concise, case-specific instructions for various types of events in the Annexes, and suitable Job Action Sheets.

Interagency Cooperation

This role is a prime candidate for interagency cooperation. Under normal circumstances, each organization which is responding to any incident will have specific elements of inventory, either in its possession or under its control, about which the other organizations have little or no knowledge. The bringing together of all of the Logistics Chiefs from all agencies into an interagency Logistics Task Force may facilitate improved access to, and flow of, resources among the participants. To illustrate, a hospital may be able to access a municipal snowplough from the Public Works department to clear the driveways and approaches to the hospital during a snowstorm, or the hospital's Dietary department may be able to establish a mass-feeding operation for first responders in the hospital cafeteria. These are but two examples, and the list of potential examples of the benefits of such a Task Force are significant.

Finance Chief

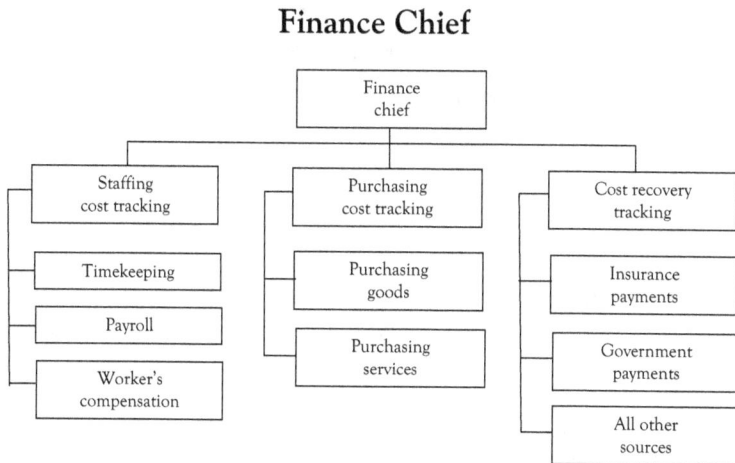

Figure 3.13 The Finance Chief with subordinate roles

Sometimes described as "Accountability" or "Administration" in some Command-and-Control models, this role is responsible for the approval, tracking, and payment of all costs associated with the response to the incident. It typically holds any petty cash resources, and it will approve any purchases or expenditures. This role is responsible for the continuous tracking of response costs of all types, and for the provision of both interim reports on costs incurred, and total costs of response to the incident.[18] Typical subordinate resources include Staffing Costs, Accounts Payable, and any Workers' Compensation issues. While it may not be necessary for the Finance role to have a continuous presence in the Command Center, they must remain readily available to consult with the Incident Manager, and their participation in the Business Cycle meetings is essential.

Selection

Every hospital has individuals who perform such functions on a daily basis. Such individuals are the obvious candidates to fill such positions during a crisis. Appropriate candidates for this position include the organization's Chief Financial Officer, supported by senior Accounting staff. Sufficient depth is required in this role to support 24-hour operations, if required. Subordinate functions are appropriately run by senior staff from the Purchasing, Accounts Payable, and Payroll departments. As with most positions, provisions should be made for the roles to be filled by "ad-hoc" staff, until predesignated staff can arrive. These would include appropriate provisions in the Emergency Response Plan, as well as appropriate Job Action Sheets.

Interagency Cooperation

Despite the fact that this role is absolutely essential to the successful operation of the Command-and-Control model and the response to the incident, it remains purely internal. There is no ongoing requirement for interagency collaboration in this function. Work with other agencies will probably be required subsequent to the conclusion of the event, particularly in dealing with various levels of government with regard to the potential recovery of the hospital or healthcare agency's response costs.

Subordinate Roles

There are, in any crisis, those who may be described as its "unsung heroes." These are often roles which do not appear in any organization chart, but they are nonetheless absolutely essential to the success of the response.[19] While the Incident Manager and the Incident Management Team will be lauded, both the smooth functioning of the Command Center which made this result possible, and the exceptional documentation of decisions, events, and actions which protect the organization after the event, are likely to be overlooked. While many unsung heroes will contribute to the response, there are two in particular which deserve special mention, and which should be predesignated.

The Scribe

In any type of major incident response, the creation of appropriate and detailed documentation is essential. Every event and action, each discussion, and every decision must be documented. This includes actions which were considered, but not enacted, and also the reasons for each decision, where possible. In most jurisdictions, if such documentation is created at the time of the event, and if that documentation was created as a duty of the individuals involved, it is highly likely that all of it will ultimately prove to be admissible in any coroner's inquest, public inquiry, criminal or civil proceeding, which may follow the event itself. Such information is also invaluable for post-event analysis and problem-solving, and for the education of both team members and other staff following the event. Additionally, the Incident Manager will require assistance with the creation of a formal, written, Incident Action Plan, periodic Situation Reports, and an After-Action Report.

As essential as all of this information is, the Incident Manager simply does not have the time to generate all of it, and still manage the incident effectively. The creation of such information is the role of the Scribe. The position of Scribe is not simply required during Business Cycle meetings; wherever possible, it should be a permanent position, and the Incident Manager and the Scribe should be "joined at the hip," virtually inseparable. The duties of the Scribe are essentially about documentation, in particular, about the creation of minutes for every meeting, whether formal or informal, that the Incident Manager attends. The Scribe should be someone with above average documentation skills; in particular, someone who is accustomed to recording the minutes of various meetings. Computer skills are essential, and, although quickly disappearing, the ability to take Shorthand notes would also be an asset. Good candidates for such a position are the Executive Assistants who normally work for the very senior members or an organization's management team. Such positions should be predesignated, with both a primary person and multiple "back-ups," in order to sustain the operation of the role during large or protracted events. While the Scribe will normally work with and report directly to the Incident Manager, the Office Manager position will normally provide administrative support.

Office Manager

Every Command Center requires someone operating discreetly in the background, ensuring that all of the systems and services operate exactly as they are supposed to; effectively and seamlessly. The simple truth is that the person in charge and the person who knows how to change the toner cartridge in the printer are rarely one and the same! The Office Manager ensures that all office equipment continues to operate effectively, ensures that telephones are answered, maintains the levels of office supplies, and coordinates the activities of those in Support Roles, so that essential maintenance and repairs can occur without any undo disruption of the Command Center business. The Office Manager should be someone whose day-to-day activities and expertise involve similar roles, and likely candidates are senior administrative staff personnel. The position, like those of the Incident Management Team, should be predesignated wherever it is possible to do so, with at least two designated "back-up" role candidates.

The role of the Office Manager is to ensure that the Incident Manager is free to concentrate on actual incident management activities, without the unnecessary distractions of the more mundane business operation requirements which are generated by every Command Center operation. There are many Command-and-Control models which have attempted to attribute such activities to the role of Scribe. Unfortunately, however, if the Scribe is doing that job correctly, there is unlikely to be sufficient "spare" time to adequately perform all of the Office Manager's duties. While not a critical position in all responses, during large or protracted responses, the presence of such a role can be an invaluable asset to the Incident Manager.

Support Roles

Many types of systems include those people who operate in the spotlight, and also those who operate quietly in the background, usually making the contributions of those in the spotlight possible. In crisis response, they are often the "unsung heroes," and while they may not be acknowledged during an actual event, it is certainly appropriate to recognize those contributions here. The following roles are not specific components of any Command-and-Control model. They are, however, support services which are essentially quite important to the successful operation of the Command-and-Control model. As such, the need for each of these services, and the source for such services during any crisis, require advance consideration by any Emergency Manager who is operating in a hospital or healthcare setting.

Security

While Security staff have day-to-day roles in virtually every hospital; there are specific requirements during any type of disaster, which will need to be considered, and provided for in advance. These will include an additional presence in the Emergency Department, and additional assignments to control unauthorized access to the Hospital Command Center, the Media Information Center, and the Family Information Center. These measures are required to prevent any disruption of essential processes such as patient treatment and decision making, which are essential to the successful response to the crisis; essentially by controlling the movement of individuals of various categories, including the media, distraught victims, and also distraught family members. It is not uncommon during any large-scale crisis for the security requirements in a hospital to double, or even triple from normal staffing levels.

Information Technology

Computers are wonderful ... when they work. Computer technology has moved the evolution of Command Centers forward dramatically in the past decade, particularly in the hospital/healthcare sector. The information which this technology can provide has become absolutely essential to the successful resolution of an incident. The problem is that, particularly in the healthcare sector, those using this technology are not what might be described as "expert" users. In order to use the technology, some level of expertise support is usually required. This is particularly true in the hospital/healthcare setting, where the Command Center is rarely purpose-built, and requires the assembly of its technologies within an improvised space.

Expertise is not only required for the assembly of the equipment. It is also required for the provision of access to an established network, or the creation of a temporary, secure network (the Command Center), whether by Ethernet or a Wi-Fi system. It is also needed for the registration and authorization of individual computers and peripherals, such as printers, on that network. Levels of authority and permitted uses of the system may also change during a crisis. Systems, which under normal circumstances severely limit Internet browsing, may need to change this for selected individuals during any crisis. Activation of disaster-specific software, or even simple repairs to computers and peripherals, may also be required.

For the computer network to be truly effective in a Command Center setting, it must appear to be as "seamless" as possible to the end users of the Incident Management Team. This is the role of Information Technology. Fortunately, most hospitals have such individuals on staff, in order to maintain the operation of their internal networks on a daily basis. In smaller organizations, such services may be provided by contractors. It is essential for the Emergency Manager to ensure that such services are available to the Command Center, either within the facility or with rapid access (within 1 hour), around the clock. Such individuals will normally fall under the supervision of the Office Manager, during any crisis or incident response.

Telecommunications

In any hospital, telecommunications systems are becoming increasingly complex. This may be further complicated, as many hospitals have migrated from conventional telephony to Voice Over Internet Protocol (VoIP) telephony, in search of operating cost savings.[20] In a purpose-built Hospital Command Center, this would be addressed by the simple, one-time, installation of the appropriate telephones, which are then left in place until needed. Most hospitals, however, do not have such a luxury, and the Hospital Command Center will occupy a multiuse, improvised space for the duration of the response. It may be possible to preinstall telephone jacks in the walls, but the actual installation of the telephones and the activation of the associated phone numbers requires specific expertise. If the hospital uses a conventional telephone system, they should have an arrangement for an emergency response by the local telephone service provider, in order to make the necessary installations. In the case of VoIP telephony, it is likely that this role has already been transferred to the hospital's Information Technology staff, or to a contracted service provider. The ongoing presence in the building, or within a maximum one-hour response time, of at least one individual with the appropriate expertise is essential to a successful Command-and-Control model.

Housekeeping

The maintenance of a stress-free environment is important, if not essential, to an effective Command-and-Control model. It has been proven that the absence of litter, and of other forms of disorganization, actually contributes to a reduction of the stress levels of a work environment. This is specifically what the hospital's Housekeeping staff does every day. The maintenance of the environment in the Hospital Command Center is probably not on the daily work schedule, and it will need to be added. Additional attention will also be required in any Breakout Rooms or staff feeding/rest areas which are associated with the Hospital Command Center operation. In addition, the required cleaning and tidying will need to be scheduled so as not to disrupt either Business Cycle meetings or other high-priority activities in the Hospital Command Center. A clean workspace is a low-stress workspace, and your Incident Management Team will thank you for it.

Dietary

In any hospital or healthcare agency which is involved in a crisis, the challenges to Dietary staff, and also their major contributions, focus on two specific areas. The first of these will be a dramatic increase in the population of the facility, which may continue over the long term. This can be a challenge with respect to planning, since most hospitals operate on a "just-in-time" basis, with respect to food delivery. This is a major potential issue, for which the Dietician may serve as an expertise resource for the Incident Manager and Logistics functions.

The second key role is the care and feeding of staff who are responding to the crisis; in particular, the Command Center staff. From personal experience, the longer an event runs, the less attractive pizza and other fast food become as eating options. Hospitals are fortunate, in that, unlike communities, they normally have trained Dieticians on staff, who can support Logistics through the creation of a feeding plan which provides variety and balanced nutrition.

Conclusion

Within any hospital or healthcare agency, the management of the response to any type of incident is always a team effort. This teamwork must flow from the Incident Manager, through the Command and General Staffs, to their subordinate staffs. Beyond those obvious roles, that teamwork must continue on to those who play often unseen but nevertheless essential support roles and services which permit the entire command and control model to function as effectively and as seamlessly as possible. Without such a coordinated effort, no Command-and-Control model, no matter how well thought out, will function to its fullest potential.

As with so many aspects of the practice of emergency management in a hospital or a healthcare facility, the key is to plan in advance for as many potential events and needs as possible. By making the appropriate assignments and arrangements, and by establishing the appropriate resources and the methodology for accessing them before the crisis begins, the Emergency Manager is much more likely to be able to ensure that the response to that crisis will be successful. Hospitals do this all the time; you have never seen a hospital wait until a patient was in a medical crisis before beginning to assemble a "crash cart." As we have learned, even the Command-and-Control model is nothing new; whether or not it has been called the Command-and-Control model, variants of this technique and its associated roles are already common within healthcare settings. Planning in a pro-active mode is almost always more effective than planning in a reactive mode. This philosophy should be reflected in the daily activities of the Emergency Manager, as well.

The key to success is for the Emergency Manager to ensure that all Incident Managers and their immediate support staff on the Incident Management Team are pre-identified wherever possible and are provided with the appropriate training and opportunities to practice the methodology. In the best traditions of emergency management, each Key Role appointment should be supported by multiple "back-up" appointments, in order to ensure both continuity and the depth required for "around the clock" and protracted operations. Specific provisions must also be made for the provision of services outside of normal business hours, through the use of "ad-hoc" staff with appropriate, pre-established, supports in place. It is, after all, a hospital, and there is a legitimate expectation that it can respond quickly and effectively to a crisis, even outside of business hours.

The development and the use of an effective Command-and-Control model can be the difference between success and failure for a hospital or a healthcare agency. To do so, the time and effort required for its creation and full development must be invested in advance, through planning, training, and ongoing dialogue with other healthcare partners and with the response agencies which, just as the hospital, serve the community. The hospital may not be considered to be a "first responder," but it is without doubt a "first receiver," and, as such, its successful application of the principles of command, control, and effective interagency coordination are likely to be an essential component of any community's response to a crisis.

Student Projects

Student Project #1

Select a healthcare-specific command and control model, either the HICS or the HECCS. Looking at the organizational chart for a particular hospital, select one primary individual and two backups for each of the Key Roles in the model. Selection should be based on knowledge, skills, and day-to-day responsibilities. Explain and defend your rationale for each selection. Ensure that your work is appropriately cited and referenced, in order to demonstrate that the appropriate level of research has occurred on this project.

Student Project #2

Select a single Key Role position, drawn from either the Command or General Staff groups. Identify all of the potential subordinate positions which might be required to support that position, in terms of its anticipated duties and role expectations. Now, looking at the organizational chart for a particular hospital, select one primary individual and two backups for each of those subordinate positions which you have already identified. Selection should be based on knowledge, skills, and day-to-day responsibilities. Explain and defend your rationale for each selection. Ensure that your work is appropriately cited and referenced, in order to demonstrate that the appropriate level of research has occurred on this project.

Test Your Knowledge

Take your time. Read each question carefully and select the MOST CORRECT answer for each. The correct answers appear at the end of the section. If you score less than 80 percent (eight correct answers) you should re-read this chapter.

1. In the Incident Command and Incident Management Systems, the group which is primarily tasked with the provision of support to the Incident Commander/Manager is called the:

(a) General Staff
(b) Command Staff
(c) Command Center Support Staff
(d) Key Roles Staff

2. The group which is primarily responsible for the provision of support to the Operations Chief is called the:

(a) General Staff
(b) Command Staff
(c) Command Center Support Staff
(d) Key Roles Staff

3. The primary advantage to the practice of predesignating those who will fill roles in the Command Center is that:

(a) Expectations are clearly understood
(b) Advance training is feasible
(c) Roles can be practiced through exercise play
(d) All of the above

4. In the early stages of a crisis, positions in the Command Center may be temporarily filled by untrained, "ad-hoc" staff through the use of:

(a) Instruction manuals
(b) On the job training
(c) Job Action Sheets
(d) All of the above

5. An arrangement in which staff from multiple agencies performing similar roles come together to an interagency response to a situation or issue is called a:

(a) Strike Team
(b) Task Force

(c) Working Group

(d) Action Team

6. In the HECCS model, support staff such as Security, Scribes, and Housekeeping, are under the supervision of the:

(a) Incident Manager

(b) Emergency Manager

(c) Office Manager

(d) Chief Scribe

7. In a Command-and-Control model, the role of the Planning Chief and subordinate staff is:

(a) The "mining" of information

(b) Analysis of information

(c) Creation of short-term plans

(d) All of the above

8. The primary role of the Incident Manager is that of:

(a) Chief strategist

(b) Chief tactician

(c) Researcher

(d) Mediator

9. In the Incident Management System and HECCS models, a unique feature of the Safety Officer role is that it may be filled by:

(a) Different individuals as the incident evolves

(b) Different individuals with specific expertise

(c) Someone from an outside agency

(d) All of the above

10. The primary responsibility of the Operations Chief in a healthcare setting is:

(a) Rescue operations

(b) Organizing the Command Center

(c) Conducting the core businesses of the organization

(d) Directing staff in disaster operations

Answers

1. (b)   2. (a)   3. (d)   4. (c)   5. (b)

6. (c)   7. (d)   8. (a)   9. (b)   10. (c)

Additional Reading

The author recommends the following exceptionally good titles as supplemental readings, which will help to enhance the student's knowledge of those topics covered in this chapter:

Canton, LG. 2007. Emergency Management: Concepts and Strategies for Effective Programs, John Wiley & Sons, New York, ISBN: 0470119756, 9780470119754

Haddow, G., J Bullock, J, Coppola, D 2013, Introduction to Emergency Management, 5th Ed., Butterworth-Heinemann, New York, ISBN: 9780124077843 eBook ISBN: 9780124104051

Lindell MK, Prater C and Perry RW 2006, Wiley Pathways Introduction to Emergency Management, 1st Ed., pp. 278, John Wiley & Sons, New York, ISBN: 978-0471772606

Molino, Jr., L.N. 2006. Emergency Incident Management Systems: Fundamentals and Applications, Wiley & Sons, New York, ISBN: 9780470043417

Purpura, P. 2011. Terrorism and Homeland Security: An Introduction with Applications, Butterworth-Heinemann, ISBN: 9780750678438, 9780080475417

USHHS 2012, What IS an Incident Action Plan?, Public Health Emergency website, operated by US Dept. of Health and Human Services, Washington, DC, www.phe.gov/Preparedness/planning/mscc/handbook/pages/appendixc.aspx (accessed March 07, 2014).

CHAPTER 4

Command Center Design

Introduction

Any healthcare facility is a complex structure, and centralized coordination of activities is essential to its operations on a daily basis. This is even more true when a disaster of any type occurs. Whether the event generates a surge in demand for services, disrupts supply chains, or forces the partial or full evacuation of the facility, strong central control is essential to the successful resolution of the incident. Municipalities, state and provincial, and federal governments understand this, and many have purpose-built facilities, or, at a minimum, a predetermined process for the assembly of such a facility, using a space which has been pre-identified and equipped in advance. Hospitals and healthcare facilities require such facilities, but the pre-identification of sites and their advance preparation are often inadequate.

This chapter will address the requirements for such a Command Center. It will examine and explore the most common designs for Command Centers which are currently in use. We will explore both the equipment and the personnel required to both run such a Center, and to provide robust supports for its operations. Operating procedures for Command Centers will be explained, including the use of the Command-and-Control model and its roles. Finally, barriers to the successful creation of such a Command Center for a healthcare facility will be explored, along with the strategies which may be used to overcome these barriers.

Learning Objectives

At the conclusion of this chapter, the student should be able to explain the role and purpose of a healthcare facility Command Center, how it operates and how its activities can be integrated with those of other healthcare partners and the community at large. The student will also understand the routine operating and reporting procedures for any type of Command Center. The student should be able to describe the various types of Command Center designs which are available for use in a healthcare facility, along with the strengths and weaknesses of each. The various roles within and supporting Command Center operations will be understood, along with the equipment and support services required to support the Command Center's operations.

Role and Purpose

The Command Center, within any type of healthcare facility, is intended to fulfill several functions. The first of these is to provide a designated meeting point and workspace in which those in charge of the response to the emergency may meet and work together in order to resolve that emergency.[1] It provides a centralized "nexus" of information flow, so that all essential information related to the emergency event flows through a single point. It must be remembered that the "currency" of disaster management is information, and that the availability of the most comprehensive and best possible information is absolutely essential to the process of making the correct decisions to guide the facility through the emergency.[2]

The operation of the Command Center also provides for a standardized and regular process by which to manage the emergency, including the gathering and distribution of resources, analysis of information, development of strategies, and coordination with other healthcare providers and outside agencies.[3] It permits the treatment of the resolution of the incident as a project, with project management skills and techniques coming into play; it ensures one plan, forging consistency and eliminating conflicting direction to staff.

The Command Center provides a single, central point upon which all individuals and agencies can rely for information and guidance.[4] There is only ONE place to take a question, or a problem, and only ONE source from which work direction flows to frontline supervisory staff. This provides tremendous consistency. It also ensures that absolutely EVERY occurrence, decision, direction, measure, or activity is thoroughly documented in a manner which will help to make such activities defensible, should this be required after the fact. A standardized, fact-based decision-making process is essential to protecting the facility from claims of malpractice or liability once the emergency is concluded. It is a process which both generates and guarantees the ability to demonstrate that, in all reasonable matters, due diligence has occurred.

Challenges to Command Center Creation

The challenges to Command Center creation within a healthcare facility are generally due to four factors. The first of these is the lack of space for purpose-built facilities. The second challenge is generally intense competition for a limited budget. The third is that the Command Center project is rarely seen as a part of the "core-business" of the facility, and is focused, at least in the minds of decision makers, on an issue which, hopefully, "might never happen." These challenges can make a Command Center project a very difficult "sell" for the Emergency Manager in a healthcare facility. Each of these will be examined independently.

The challenge of space availability is often due to the fact that space within a given hospital or healthcare facility is generally at a premium, and the competition for such spaces by competing departments is generally intense. Space usage within hospitals is generally driven by the evolution of medical technologies. Given the high cost of new construction, the process tends to be limited to the existing four walls of the hospital building, and the competition within that space becomes intense. Generally speaking, a given iteration of technology, a CT scanner, for example, usually has a useful life expectancy of about five to seven years, before advances in technology render it less than "state of the art."

Such devices are generally on a plan, at least in the minds of the users, of scheduled replacement. One of the challenges with this is that in order to maintain services while the technology is upgraded, it is generally necessary to install the new technology in a second space, while the older technology continues to provide service until the new equipment is completely tested and ready to replace it. For this reason, even when a given space might appear to be available, there is an excellent chance that some Department has already earmarked it for their next round of expansion.

It may be prudent to at least attempt to look at the expansion and service relocation plans of various departments, and to attempt to secure a space which one of them is already planning on vacating; this is much less likely to incite resistance to space allocation, particularly when they were already planning on vacating the space. It is also likely that a multipurpose space, usable on a daily basis as a classroom or a boardroom, and quickly convertible into a Command Center, is much more likely to be well received, than a proposal for a full-time, dedicated facility.

Budget is another of the challenges with approval of a Command Center project. Whether publicly or privately funded, healthcare facilities have limited financial resources, and, as with space allocation, the competition for these resources is usually quite intense. Most evolution of healthcare facility space usage tends to be project-driven, and in most cases, Department Heads are masters at this process. They are aware of the evolution rates in their respective technologies, and usually operate their own project/proposal timelines based upon the known rate of technological evolution. As a result, the creation of the research required to craft an appropriate proposal for the next project, including space allocation and budget, generally begins within days of the latest iteration of the technology beginning to operate.

Such proposals tend to be extremely detailed, with explanations of technology, projected service demands, needs assessments, and risk management decisions, all supported by immaculate research, and all in place as a highly credible and concrete proposal, before the document ever sees the light of day. The combination of these factors mean that it can be difficult to persuade the allocation of such space for a dedicated project which, even the Emergency Manager hopes, will be used only rarely. This is particularly true when the Emergency Manager crafts their own proposals on the old-fashioned "what-if" scenarios, instead of using the comprehensive research and project planning skills used by their competitors. The only real solution to these problems is for the Emergency Manager operating in a healthcare setting to acquire the same essential skills, such as applied research methodology and project management,[5] Lean for Healthcare and Six Sigma, and to apply these diligently, in order to produce proposals which are of competitive quality.

Design Types

Command Centers may consist of purpose-built facilities, which are somewhat rare in the healthcare setting. They may also be improvised facilities, or a hybrid combination of these two factors. When not purpose-built, they may function on a "push" or a "pull" assembly process. There are a variety of potentially effective design layouts, and a number of support facilities, resources, and staff which will be required. Each of these factors will be explored in detail in the following pages.

Purpose-Built

A purpose-built Command Center is a dedicated space in which all of the elements and technologies required to manage an emergency remain assembled and operational on an ongoing basis. All that is normally required is for the Command Team to report to the designated facility and begin the management process. Such facilities usually maintain a rota of on-call Duty Officers, whose job is to ensure that all resources and equipment are in place, regularly tested, and ready for use. The Duty Officers may also perform an active monitoring function regarding events happening nearby and likely to affect the Command Center. Such facilities are fairly common among large cities and the higher levels of government, but are something of a rarity in healthcare, for reasons which have already been discussed.

While such Command Centers are the ideal, they are also difficult to justify in terms of expense, except in a very large organization. Consider the cost of purchasing a dozen or more computers and peripherals, assembling them in a network, and then never using them other than for training purposes or an actual emergency! This is typically beyond the means of small municipalities, to say nothing of the budget challenges which would face a hospital. Such dedicated facilities are not at all portable, and when one considers that one of the fundamental principles of emergency management is multiple layers of redundancy, it may well be that building an expensive dedicated primary Command Center but lacking the funding for a similar off-site backup Command Center, is a relatively perilous risk management choice.

Improvised

An improvised Command Center employs some other facility which has another purpose in daily use, and which is only occasionally converted to Command Center usage. The equipment required for Command Center usage is either securely stored within the designated space, or is securely stored elsewhere, and requires transportation to the improvised site. In either case, the resources required, including computers and peripherals, telephones, radios, televisions (TVs), office supplies, and occasionally, even furniture, will require assembly, testing, and in some cases, connection to a network, whether computer or telephone, before they can be used. These are typical in smaller municipal governments and also quite commonly used in hospitals and other types of healthcare facilities. In a healthcare setting, such improvised settings typically employ boardrooms, hospital classrooms, or similar locales.[6] While they do require assembly time (how much depends on how you design them) and technical support to operate, they tend to be much less expensive, since a great deal of the equipment, and certainly the space, are being used for other purposes on a daily basis. The most significant advantage to this design approach is the ability to simply pick up and move all equipment to a back-up operating site, should the use of the primary site be denied by the effects of the incident.[7]

Hybrid

A hybrid Command Center is a design in which the principles of an Improvised design still apply, but one in which much of the underlying infrastructure has been put in place in advance. The room may look to all who see it as a very ordinary, everyday boardroom or classroom. However, concealed in the walls and ceiling are additional telephone lines and jacks, emergency electrical power plugs, a wireless router for the computer network, and so on. The room may also have wall or ceiling mounted flat screen monitors, which are used on a daily basis for teaching, but which readily convert to display essential information to Command Center staff, when required. Such facilities often also provide for the discreet, secure storage of all other Command Center supplies.

Such Command Center designs can typically activate much more quickly than the traditional Improvised approach, because they are essentially "plug and play." They are considerably more difficult, however, to relocate, should the use of the primary site chosen be denied to the Command Center staff (e.g., fire). In any multiuse facility, the space will require regular monitoring and clarification of "ownership," since it is not uncommon for other users to assume that since they use the space regularly, they can re-allocate such items as telephone lines, or place an essential daily system on the computer network router in the room, without any prior consultation.

"Push" Systems

An assembly system for either the Improvised or Hybrid model in which essential Command Center equipment is stored elsewhere in a secured location and then brought to the assembly site when required is called a "push" system. Such systems typically employ a locked box system (one or more boxes for each function in the Command Center) in which boxes of equipment are inventoried, then sealed, and placed where no one has access to them other than for inspection purposes, and in which any attempted interference with the contents will be immediately evident.

The contents of each box will vary according to the role of the individual using it. In any IMS-based command and control model, for example, the box for the Logistics Chief is likely to contain a list of essential equipment and resource suppliers, along with 24-hour contact instructions. Similar boxes would exist for each role, and for any other essential Command Center staff. Other boxes might contain a "starter kit" of essential office supplies and blank forms upon which the Command Center will operate.

In such Command Center kits, these boxes are typically secured inside of lock-able wheeled carts, which are themselves secured within a locked space. Access to these locked spaces is limited, usually to only the Emergency Manager and to hospital Security. This permits the monthly inspection of the kit, without making it available for "pilfering" by those who believe that they require the equipment more than the kit does. When requested, the cart(s) are simply removed from their secured space by Security or some other group and brought to the designated assembly space, where they are then unloaded, and the Command Center assembled. Once empty, the boxes and carts are returned to their secure storage location, where they are out of the way.

The biggest single advantage of such a system is its portability. It can be readily transported to the predesignated site. However, should the nature of the emergency deny the use of that site, it can be readily transported to an alternate operating site elsewhere on the campus. It can even be simply loaded onto a truck or van and relocated to a designated off-site alternate operating location, should events dictate that this step is needed. This permits healthcare facilities to embrace the principle of multiple layers of redundancy.

"Pull" Systems

In some Improvised, and many Hybrid Command Center designs, a system in which all of the required Command Center supplies are kept in locked cabinets within the designated space is generally called a "Pull" system. The boxes themselves may be similar to the "Push" system, or they may consist of a single, locked cupboard for each essential role in the Command Center. When required, the cupboards are simply unlocked, the equipment "pulled" out, and assembled. While this results in faster assembly and activation of the Command Center, its lack of portability generally precludes the use of the equipment at an alternate operating site, should this be needed. That being said, the author has seen one particularly inspired design in which the wheeled carts were locked in a closet in the designated space, providing the best elements of both design approaches.

Design Considerations

The Command Center is, by definition, a high-stress environment. Given that most of the occupants are likely to be "Type A" personalities, and already under elevated levels of pressure, any design approaches which can be used to mitigate stress levels will be essential to the successful use of the site. General principles of ergonomics do apply,[8] and if an ergonomist is available, they can make substantial contributions to the design of the environment. At a minimum, lighting, heat and air exchange, ambient noise levels, comfort of workspaces, and security are essential elements to consider.[9]

With respect to lighting, this factor can, by itself, significantly reduce stress levels for the occupants of the Command Center. At a minimum, try to avoid the use of blue-spectrum lighting, whether fluorescent or compact fluorescent, as this has been demonstrated in studies to elevate stress levels. Full-spectrum or yellow-spectrum systems have been proven to be less stressful. Consider the potential for variable level lighting, if available. This can be used to eliminate the stresses caused by continual high light level exposure on the effects of the natural Circadian rhythm. Dim the lights during evening hours, if the operation is around the clock. Ensure that the individual task lighting provided for each designated workspace is sufficient to eliminate unnecessary eye strain, while remaining adjustable to personal preferences.

The ideal work environment is neither too hot nor too cold, and should be, if possible, adjustable to individual preferences. Always bear in mind that those assigned to work in this space may very well be there for an extended period of time. While short-term discomfort can be overlooked, long-term issues of environmental comfort will affect cooperation and collaboration. Other factors which are equally essential are humidity and air exchange rates. An environment which is too humid is clearly uncomfortable, and poor air exchange results in poor air quality and a "stuffy" environment which may even contribute to conflict between the occupants of the room.

Consider the effects of ambient noise on the ability of participants to share information and collaborate. Have you ever been in a large meeting which was poorly run, in which multiple conversations were occurring at the same time, and where external noise to tended to wash out the amount which you could actually hear? Consider the need for breakout rooms for sidebar conversations. Also ensure that any telephone in the Command Center is equipped with the ability to turn off the ringer, and to rely instead of a flasher to identify incoming calls. That being said, no telephone in a Command Center should EVER be equipped with voicemail; every phone must be answered by a human being in order to ensure that no essential information is overlooked or delayed, even during a Business Cycle meeting. TV screens, while they provide essential information, should have the volume switched off, and closed captioning employed. When dynamic monitoring is essential, it should occur in a location away from the main Command Center space. Similarly, when monitoring two-way radio communications (e.g., emergency services), this activity should occur away from the main Command Center.

Consider the ergonomics of the individual workspaces. Have you ever had to sit on a hard wooden chair for an extended period of time, or had to work on a work surface which was either too high or too low, or poorly lit? Consider the effects of such variables on the occupants of the Command Center over a period of DAYS. Wherever it is possible to do so, individual chairs and work surfaces, while they cannot be personalized, should at least be adjustable. While the main meeting table in the Command Center is of a fixed height, this can and should be avoided in those spaces where staff are working between meetings. Also ensure that provisions are in place to regularly clean and maintain the Command Center, even while operations are ongoing. While coffee and drinks can be permitted, actual eating should occur elsewhere, away from the stressful environment. Similarly, waste baskets should be emptied, and work surfaces wiped down regularly. A clean and healthy environment can go a long way toward the reduction of stress levels for the occupants of the Command Center.

Security of the Command Center is also an essential issue requiring consideration. The access to the Command Center should be available ONLY to those who are actually working in it. There is an old adage among Emergency Managers which says that three categories of people will come to a Command Center; those who are assigned to it, those who are certain that they have something essential to contribute, and the tourists! Nothing will disrupt the business flow of a Command Center more quickly than large numbers of individuals wandering in and out, destroying the flow of the Business Cycle. Subordinate staff, and for that matter, unassigned superiors, should be denied entry, and, if their information is important enough, met in the corridor or a breakout room. Nothing should be permitted to disrupt the Command Center process. This does not mean that the Command Center is not accountable to the senior administration of the facility; simply that the required reporting should occur elsewhere, and at a time when it does not interfere with the management of the incident.

Another key factor of Security is the access to sensitive information. Where possible, try to avoid ground floor level meeting spaces, particularly those with large exterior windows. While natural light is a highly desirable feature for the comfort of occupants, it also provides a potential opportunity for curious members of the media to access any information posted on boards or walls, using cameras with long lenses, or to eavesdrop on your Command Center conversations using parabolic microphone technology which actually uses the vibration of the window to hear what is being said inside! As another factor, consider banning the use of personal cellular telephones in the Command Center, as most of these can be eavesdropped upon by the media. For sensitive information, ONLY landline telephones should be used. The same issues apply to both e-mail and text messages from cellular phones and some types of tablet computers.

No Command Center design is perfect, and each must, first and foremost, meet the needs of the organization creating it. In the end, the initial design will focus, in large measure, on the Emergency Manager's best estimate of the organization's needs from such a facility at the time of its creation.[10] The growth and development of such a facility will be organic, often evolving each time that it is used, as weaknesses and shortcomings are identified, as technologies evolve, and sometimes, as the role of the organization using it evolves and changes.

Layouts

The first element which should dictate your choice of Command Center layouts is the Command-and-Control model which the facility elects to use. There are a number of different physical layouts which are used in typical Command Centers or Emergency Operations Centers of various types. At this point, the student will probably benefit from a review of Chapter 1, which deals with specific Command-and-Control models, with the review focusing upon the Hospital Incident Command System and Healthcare Emergency Command and Control System models. A further review of Chapter 3 in order to refresh the student's memory on specific roles within each model will also be useful. While a number of different model layouts are presented here in order to provide examples of various options, it should be remembered that the specialized requirements and restrictions of the healthcare setting have traditionally resulted in a choice of some variation on the "Boardroom" layout.

"Mission Control"

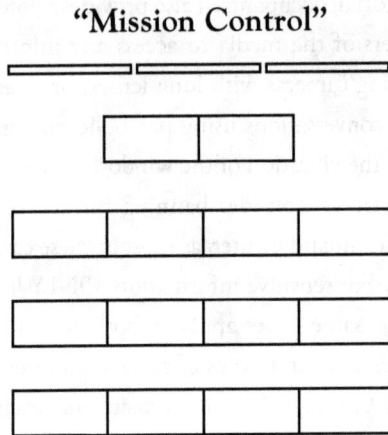

Figure 4.1 Mission control

The "Mission Control" layout is most often used in the Emergency Operations Centers of large Provincial and State Emergency Operations Centers. In this model, the layout is built around the ability to display critical information in front of the entire group, both with whiteboards, and, above these, flat screen TV screens, which can be used to display a variety of information, including data, PowerPoint presentations, videoconferencing with other sites, live TV coverage, and Internet-based information such as weather displays. As technology becomes more advanced, it is likely that live images from the scene of the incident, provided by either hand-held camera, "smart" phones or tablets, or even aerial drones, will become practical and feasible.

In this model, the Incident Manager and the Scribe are seated, facing all other members of the Command Team (Public Information, Liaison, Safety, Operations, Planning, Logistics, and Finance). Each of these is seated at their own workstation, with the ability to add information from their own computers to the overhead screens, to be viewed by the entire Team. By arranging the workstations in this manner, Team members do not need to relocate in order to attend a Business Cycle meeting. They simply look up and participate. Additional seating is provided for use by the Office Manager, Senior Management Team observers, and observers from outside agencies.

This layout is one of the older designs and was originally driven by the need for low profile linear connection of telecommunications, computer network, and power cabling. In doing so, it creates an environment which is very "information-rich," without interfering in the team communications processes. The model requires a large, dedicated room, and typically provides more seating and workspaces than would be typically required by any healthcare facility. It is still used by larger government agencies, and by, among others, NASA.

"Marketplace"

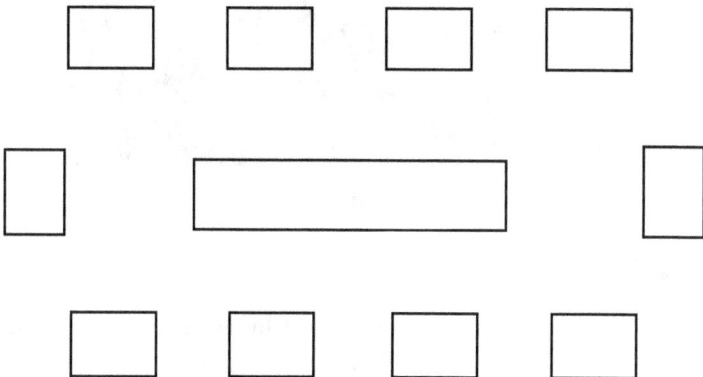

Figure 4.2 The "Marketplace" configuration

The "Marketplace" layout is typically found in improvised Command Centers and Emergency Operations Centers which are deployed in improvised spaces in smaller communities. These are often located in school gymnasia and municipal recreation centers, where the space starts as a "blank canvas," with no wiring or cabling, and where everything must be set up "from scratch." In this model, each key role in the Command-and-Control model "owns" one table or workspace, and individuals typically move from table to table, negotiating access to resources or other types of collaboration. When a Business Cycle meeting occurs, those in key roles typically gather around the large central table for the actual meeting. The challenge with such configurations includes the ability to share electronic information as a group, and the physical hazards associated with widespread electrical and telecommunications cabling, leading to trip and fall hazards, and the ability to disconnect all or a significant part of the entire system by simply tripping over the wrong cable. Such systems are also connected to emergency power sources only rarely, making them even more vulnerable. This particular design layout is rapidly falling from favor.

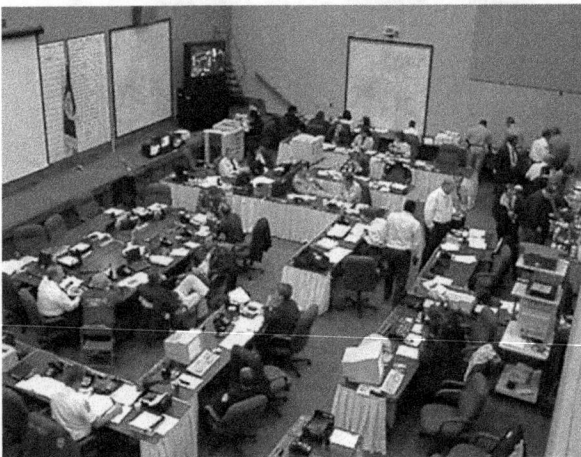

A typical marketplace configuration

"Bull's-Eye"

The Bull's Eye layout is most often used by larger cities which have chosen to use their local Council's meeting chambers as an improvised Emergency Operations Center. This permits the seating of the Incident Manager at the center of the "Bull's Eye" with all other Command Team staff arranged in a circle around him or her. It provides an additional advantage in that staff who are supporting either the Command Center or individual members of the Command Team may occupy the outer ring of the configuration as observers, can take notes or pass relevant information to their own Supervisors, who are actually participating in the meeting. Such systems have an advantage, in that all prewiring and cabling, emergency power and audiovisual displays are already incorporated into the layout because of its everyday uses. This model is most commonly used in larger cities, but may also be occasionally found in larger, university-affiliated teaching hospitals, who may employ a lecture hall for this use.

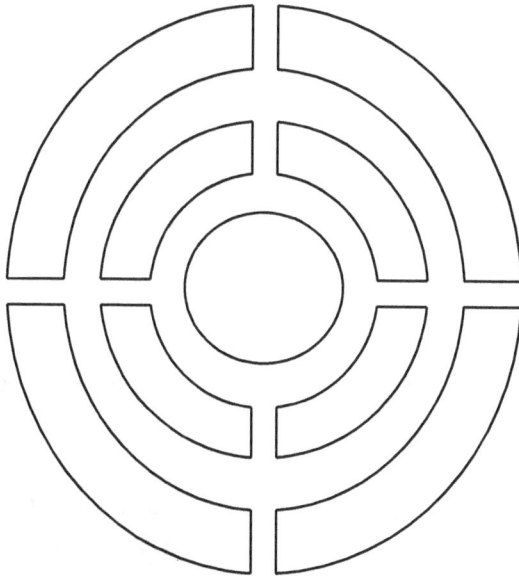

Figure 4.3 The "Bull's Eye"

City Council Chambers, located in the City of Hamilton, Canada performs double duty as the Municipal Command Center

"Boardroom"

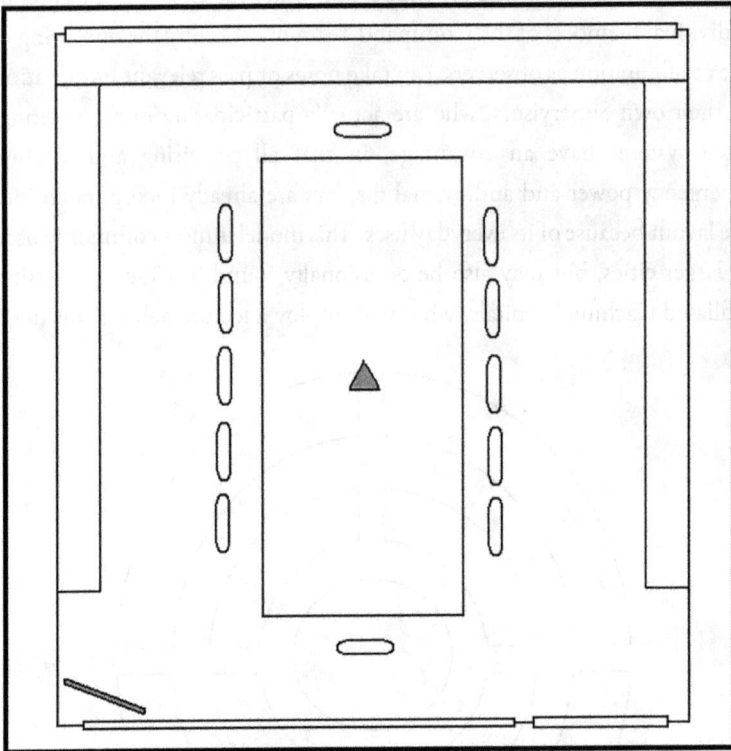

Figure 4.4 The "Boardroom"

The Boardroom layout is the most common configuration for Command Centers within healthcare settings. This usually consists of an adaptation of the hospital's existing boardroom for the purposes of running the emergency. This configuration permits a good deal of audiovisual display, both on screens and on overhead video display. It also often includes videoconferencing equipment. If the boardroom has been well designed, emergency power is already present. In this model, the Incident Manager sits at the head of the table, usually with the Scribe at the opposite end. In between, all members of the Command Team are seated, along with any other interested parties or observers. A well-designed facility can include "invisible" low-profile workstations (gate-leg, fold up, resemble a chair rail) along the side walls, where Command Team members can work between Business Cycle meetings. In some cases, these are not included, and Command Team members work in their regular workspaces, subject to recall by the Incident Manager. Such facilities are already equipped with clerical support and office equipment, washrooms, and often, even a kitchenette. In some cases, even "artwork" is reversible, with whiteboards on the other side. By day, a prestigious boardroom, but by night ... the Command Center. This layout is often the easiest "sell" for the Emergency Manager; most facilities require such a room in any case, and the multiple uses ensure lower operating costs. This is a classic example of an Emergency Manager considering multiple users in order to achieve a required objective.

The Emergency Operations Center, Deer Park, Texas. A typical "Boardroom" configuration. Note the individual workstations for the Command Team built into the walls

"Virtual"

A good deal of attention has been paid to the concept of the "virtual" Command Center. This is a logical follow-on of the software industry's efforts to provide virtual conferencing and may very well be the "wave of the future." At the moment, however, such systems typically lack the type of robust information sharing that occurs in a physical Command Center. They are also relatively insecure, with hackers, including, in some cases, the media, able to readily eavesdrop, if they know which system you are using. Finally, such systems typically rely on either the Internet services provided by local cable TV companies or telephone providers, or on the cellular telephone network. All of these systems are potentially subject to disruption by the effects of some types of emergencies, making such systems less robust than one might wish. That being said, they can be a useful tool for faster activation of the Command Center after hours, with half of the Command Team simply logging on and beginning to work from home when notified, while the other half proceed to the physical Command Center and begin activation. Once they are active, the virtual work from home is transferred, and the second half of the team reports to the physical Command Center. The flaws in such systems are continually improving; we are simply "not there" yet.

Information Display

Most modern Command Centers are designed around the ability to display information to the entire group. What was once a single, old-technology vacuum tube TV in one corner of the room has quickly become enhanced, multi-image display, with the ability to display information from several sources simultaneously? Most modern Command Centers are built around either a single projection screen at one end of the room (and this is becoming obsolete) or a bank of flat-screen monitors, typically in the 42-in. range, arranged near the ceiling at the head of the room, or, when money is no object, around the entire room. Such screens can be used to permit videoconferencing, information from local broadcast news sources, Internet-based data such as weather forecasts, CCTV footage from your own facility, or presentations such as PowerPoint and other types of data from various members of the Command Team. Ideally, such screens are volume controlled, in order to eliminate unacceptable levels of ambient noise, with dialogue typically replaced by closed captioning.

In the most elaborate versions of such displays, a touch-sensitive screen is configured as a tabletop, with a base (raster) layer of the community map or institutional floor plan, and the potential to overlay literally hundreds (how many depends on you) of layers of additional information, in order to see relationships between data sets and to employ these for planning purposes. In the most elaborate versions of such tools, viewers can actually overlay real-time information, such as the GPS-based tracking of moving emergency vehicles, with other types of information, such as a plane crash location, flood waters, forest fires, population centers, and so on.

The more basic versions of such technology are no longer particularly expensive, although the system just described might cost tens of thousands of dollars. Digital TVs have largely replaced the old vacuum tube devices, which are obsolete, difficult to repair, and should be replaced at the earliest opportunity. Also, flat screen technology is more amenable to the conversion from analog to digital TV signals, which is currently well underway around the world. The more modern flat screen TVs have actually become less expensive than the older technology. Increasingly, "smart" TVs, based upon the Android operating system, can provide an entirely new depth to displayed information, with multi-image display, and incorporating live TV signals, closed circuit TV images, computer-generated images and data, and videoconferencing. The ability to display large volumes of information from various sources can be accomplished with relative ease, using your institution's own information technology professionals, and such arrangements should be made as simple and user friendly as possible.

Some of the technologies which, at this writing are literally just over the horizon, are the ability to monitor your own facility and property from the air, using small, inexpensive, unmanned drone aircraft. Some emergency services are also experimenting with this technology, and it may soon be possible to actively observe the effects of a communitywide emergency in your own Command Center, using Internet-based video feeds from your local emergency services. The key to all of this is to buy the best technology that you can afford for your Command Center; it is likely to remain current longer and will do far more than bargain-priced equipment.

Telephony

Telephones are an essential component to any Command Center operation; the currency of disaster management is information, and telephones are often the primary and most reliable source. When establishing a Command Center, there are fundamental elements of telephone technology which the Emergency Manager needs to understand and employ in the planning process.[11] In order to address this, we will examine each type of telephone technology, along with its relative strengths and weaknesses. We will begin with the elements of a telephone handset, then examine how networks work, and finally, examine different types of telephony technology.

The first thing which the Emergency Manager needs to understand is that old-fashioned analog telephones draw their operating power from the telephone line, while modern digital telephones, despite all of their push buttons and flashing lights, do not. When power goes out, analog telephones should continue to operate, while only those digital telephones which are connected to emergency power sources will continue to operate. When designing the Command Center, since digital telephones are almost exclusively the choice of handset, it is essential to ensure that there are enough emergency power outlets in the Command Center to provide power to the telephones, in addition to everything else. As a variation on the theme of multiple layers of redundancy, it is always a good idea to keep a few analog telephones around.

Local handsets in the Command Center should be equipped with flashers to indicate incoming calls, and with the ability to silence the ringer, in order to reduce ambient noise levels in the Command Center. No telephone in a Command Center should EVER be equipped with Voice Mail … there is a natural and unfortunate tendency to ignore phones during meetings and let Voice Mail deal with them. The problem with this is that access to critical information can be lost, or at minimum, substantially delayed; phones should ALWAYS be answered in a Command Center, even during the Business Cycle meetings.

The Emergency Manager should also consider blocking the outgoing Caller ID function on all telephones in the Command Center and instituting a single number for incoming calls. This provides a single point of contact, which can be monitored, and the calls transferred accordingly, regardless of what is happening in the Command Center, and permits the taking of messages. Blocking outgoing Caller ID ensures that every number in the Command Center does not become an incoming line, as people become aware of the number. This way, Command Center staff will always have access to protected outgoing lines with which to conduct their business and work direction.

Cellular telephones (tele mobiles) are NOT a suitable substitute for landline telephones. Bear in mind the principle in emergency management of multiple layers of redundancy, with each backup system being technologically independent of the system which it is intended to replace.

A cellular telephone is simply a two-way radio from the user to the nearest cellular tower; beyond that, the system relies on the same telephone network as every conventional telephone in the hospital. If one isn't working, the other won't work either! Satellite telephones are a suitable replacement but tend to be hideously expensive to acquire and use. As a result, while having a few is a good idea, ensure that you have suitable controls on their use.

Increasingly, hospitals and other healthcare facilities are moving away from conventional telephony, and toward Voice over Internet Protocol (VoIP) telephony for their internal networks. This is driven, in large measure, by the cheaper operating costs of VoIP systems. This means that the hospital telephone network is directly dependent on the same internal IT network, and on the hospital's Internet service provider. When computer networks go down, phones do as well, and vice-versa. If the Emergency Manager has any input into such decisions, your facility should be encouraged to maintain at least a few conventional telephone lines, providing a backup system which is technologically independent of your primary telephone system.

Other things to know about telephones, include the pay telephones located in most hospital lobbies and Emergency Departments. Even when the hospital converts to VoIP, these telephones, which do not belong to the hospital, but to the telephone service provider, will generally continue to operate even when the VoIP system has failed. Even when the facility is still using conventional telephony, such phones are often on a different exchange from the rest of the building. The simple truth is that the local telephone company has two types of revenue: monthly bills and fee for service. Monthly bills get paid whether the service is interrupted or not, while fee for service systems, such as pay telephones or long-distance services, generate no revenue when not in use. The telephone companies understandably repair these systems first! A telephone dial tone is a courtesy signal ... it is NOT essential for the telephone to operate. As a result, if the line seems dead, try dialling anyway ... it might just work! Also, if no other telephone in the building is working, try the pay phones. Finally, even when a local call will not go through, try a long-distance call ... they are separate systems, and in most telephone companies, long distance service is typically repaired first.

Radios

When considering radios, there are two separate and distinct approaches which must be considered. Each has its own uses, and each will be considered separately. The first of these is the use of simple radio receivers to monitor the events which have generated the emergency. This may consist of commercial radio and TV news coverage, or it may employ digital scanner-type devices to actively monitor (with permission) emergency services radio frequencies. The second is the use of two-way radios for actual communications. These may be the facility's own radios, usually walkie-talkies, or may bring the facility into a more elaborate communications network.

The monitoring of commercial radio and TV for information about an emergency is a long-standing practice, but one which is gradually disappearing. At one time, the local radio station was staffed around the clock, had its own newsroom and reporters, and provided information to the community in real time. Those in emergency management, and in the local hospital, could actually call the station and ask them to broadcast requests for off-duty staff to report to work and so on. This was seen as a part of the station's community service obligation. As technology has evolved, local radio stations have been forced to evolve as well, as a matter of survival.

In many cases, certainly in smaller centers, but in some cases, in larger centers as well, the "local" radio station has become partly or fully automated. Music and programming, including news coverage, are purchased from a national service, and the last part of the station to actually operate locally may well be advertising sales. Unless your emergency makes national news, you will hear nothing about it on your local station, and broadcasting requests for staff to report to work, or asking the public to avoid an overwhelmed Emergency Department are now technically impossible. For this reason, it is essential for the Emergency Manager to engage in dialogue with the local radio station(s), in order to understand exactly how they work, and what they can and cannot do. If the local station is fully automated, there is little point to monitoring it.

The monitoring of TV stations can be helpful to obtain information regarding external emergencies. That being said, it must be remembered that this is true only of local TV stations. Unless a disaster makes national news coverage, no information is likely to appear on national sources, such as CNN (United States), CBC News Network (Canada), or BBC News (UK), and if it does appear, it is often two or more hours out of date, and therefore of little interest in the management of the incident. In those cases, in which the TV station provides regional coverage, but is not located in the same community as the hospital, the Emergency Manager should anticipate at least a one-hour delay before any meaningful coverage commences, bearing in mind that reporters and camera crews must physically travel to the incident before they can begin to cover it.

The passive monitoring of radio and TV sources can generate significant amounts of ambient noise. For this reason, it is desirable to have a separate monitoring facility, some distance from the Command Center, so as not to generate a distraction to the business of the Command Center.[12] The monitoring of media coverage can logically be assigned to the Public Information Officer and subordinates, who should probably be listening to the coverage in any case. If local TV news coverage is to be displayed in the Command Center itself, this should occur with the volume off, and closed captioning in place.

Two-way radio communications provide some additional depth of preparedness.[13] Within the facility, they can provide a backup communications system for the telephone network, which is technologically independent of that network, eliminating or reducing the need for runners, in the event of a telephone network failure. In some locales, including both the cities of Ottawa and Toronto in Canada, private networks have been created, employing separate channels on the municipal EMS system's Ultra High Frequency trunking radio networks. These networks provide major healthcare stakeholders, including hospitals, municipally operated long-term care facilities, and Public Health, with a robust backup method of maintaining communications and coordination between network members, even in the event of a regionwide telephone network failure. Other potential sources for this type of backup may include local amateur radio operators, who, if present in the community, may be very interested in providing this service. There are specific amateur radio organizations which deal with emergency communications, including the Amateur Radio Emergency Service in Canada and the United States,[14] and RAYNET in the UK.[15]

When considering the use of two-way radio communications to support the Command Center, there are several factors which must be considered. Such systems will require an emergency power source, and this will, to some extent, dictate where such a facility can be located. Location will also be influenced by the fact that, like any other two-way radio, an antenna will be required. Such arrangements are generally made in advance, with the emergency power, antenna and antenna cabling preinstalled within a designated space, permitting the radio operator what amounts to a "plug and play" installation, when they arrive to assist the facility. It should also be noted that, as with passive radio monitoring, such systems do generate considerable levels of ambient noise. As a result, they should be located far enough away from the Command Center that their operating noise does not generate a distraction.

Information Technology and Network

The biggest single challenge to the development of a Command Center within a healthcare setting is potentially the acquisition and maintenance of the computers and peripherals which make up the information technology network.[16] Such equipment is expensive, and the rate of technological evolution, and therefore, replacement, is very fast indeed. While it would be ideal for such equipment to be for dedicated use in the Command Center, the sheer cost of such a decision would be enormous, as would the ongoing maintenance requirements for equipment which was rarely used. As with the configuration of the Command Center itself, it is often best to ensure that as much of the network as possible is multiuse, thereby offsetting the acquisition and maintenance costs.

The first element of such a system is the individual computer itself. These should be standard throughout the network, and ideally, should be of the laptop type. Desktop systems are becoming increasingly obsolete and will rarely meet the actual day-to-day needs of the user, in any case. Tablets, on the other hand, while attractive from the perspective of both size and cost, do not yet have the capacity for day-to-day business use. A good laptop computer can do literally anything that a desktop can do with respect to daily business use, with the added advantage of being fully portable, and often, more favorably priced.

In many healthcare facilities, a program to replace desktop systems of executives and senior managers with laptops is probably already underway or has occurred. This measure should be encouraged by the Emergency Manager. As a general practice, it is often best to purchase the most expensive laptop model that can be afforded; the price of such units tends to drop as their time on the market increases, and therefore, the more expensive models typically will not require replacement as soon. This approach generally holds true for network peripherals, as well.

The model of computer selected should be standardized. There is sometimes a tendency among senior managers to attempt to use laptops as yet another "badge of office," and the development of a competition to see who can acquire the most elaborate computer. This is an expensive and unnecessary approach and should be discouraged. Simply put, the more elaborate the computer, the more likely it is to require individualized support, and buying the best computers that can be afforded will almost always provide all of the features and services which are legitimately required.

In this manner, the entire system is composed of interchangeable components, and, from a hardware perspective, any computer can be replaced by any other. All computers should be equipped with Wi-Fi capability (increasingly becoming a standard feature), and each should have the ability to access the mobile telephone network in emergency circumstances, if required. All such devices come with their own chargers, but a spare battery may be required, if you ever anticipate extended usage times in no power environments.

If the use of services such as Skype are anticipated, the use of a headset is desirable, both to provide privacy and to eliminate the ambient noise for others in the Command Center. The ability to regularly back up data on the machine, by means of either a high-volume flash drive or a portable hard drive, is also recommended. All such items should fit together into a single, well-organized kit, often in its own carrying case, so that where the team member goes, so goes the computer, thereby ensuring availability in an emergency.

Virtually all organizations place some restrictions on corporately owned computers, on the types of software and the uses to which they can be put. This is completely reasonable and affects both security and appropriate usage. There is always a standard operating system (often Windows), along with a standardized suite of office tools, most often Microsoft Office. Other essential features for daily use include both an Internet browser of some type (there are several good ones) and some type of security software to protect the system from viruses and other types of malwares. On a more individual level, certain types of software or applications are sometimes banned from corporate networks. These often include social media sites, such as Facebook, Twitter, Pinterest, and so on, and the ban is the result of a decision that the use of such media is not really an appropriate use of either a business computer, or the employee's work time.

While such a configuration is fine for day-to-day use, the employee, as a Command Team member, may very well require access to resources during a crisis which are specifically banned for day-to-day usage. One example of this might be the need of the Public Information Officer to monitor what the public is saying about the emergency, or the hospital's role in it, on social media, such as Twitter. They may even need to disseminate information to the public using this avenue. There are also other tools, such as hazardous materials reference tools as one example, which are of little use on a day-to-day basis but could prove essential during a crisis. It is entirely possible, working with the IT department, to create a system in which each computer has a standardized login, which provides access to the normal business tools, and a second, secure log-in, which logs the machine in at a different level, with on screen access to a more expanded set of tools required to manage the emergency. The employee does not even receive the log-in instructions until notified of the emergency, and so, the security of the corporate network is maintained. A conversation with senior staff can show how easy this step is to accomplish.

Computer peripherals are another consideration. Wherever possible, such devices should be wireless, and a backup device should be readily available for each primary device. Examples which may be useful in a Command Center setting include printers, flatbed scanners, fax machines, photocopiers,[17] and projectors. The advent of a multipurpose device, in industry parlance an "all-in-one," can greatly simplify this process. Such systems typically combine all of the above devices, except the projector, in a single unit, and the costs of such units is very low; often less than

$100/unit at this writing. Such devices require appropriate cabling, paper, and printer ink cartridges, which are usually specific to the device itself. Each such device should have an identical replacement version, readily available nearby. It should be borne in mind that while such devices can be extremely useful in a Command Center setting, they are not intended for heavy commercial use, lacking the capacity for large-scale document production, for example. Access to larger commercial photocopiers and printers will continue to be required.

The development of a formal individual network for the Command Center will also be required. This provides a system which is independent of the main facility network and can be both more robust and more secure. Such systems can be hardwired, but this specifically eliminates the portability of the Command Center. More typically, such systems are wireless. The system will require one wireless router device with sufficient capacity to carry 10 computers and an appropriate range of peripheral devices. This router must be connected to both the emergency power supply and via Ethernet cabling to the Internet Service Provider's network. While the Command Center itself is portable, the router is not; one router will be required for the primary Command Center site, and for each designated backup operating location. Advance work with the IT department will ensure that all of the required networking of devices can occur automatically (indeed, the entire system can and should be "plug and play"), and that the appropriate network security safeguards are in place.

Conclusion

An effective Command Center can greatly enhance the ability of any healthcare organization to effectively coordinate both service delivery and resources during any crisis. The size, type, location, and equipment of this type of resource will differ from one facility to the next, as all are driven by the specific needs of the facility. This is also true of the equipment and resources which should be made available within the Command Center. What is the Command Center intended to do? For whom? Under which circumstances? There is a vast difference between the requirements of a major general hospital attempting to coordinate the reception of victims from a mass-casualty incident, and a long-term care facility attempting to perform a controlled evacuation of 200 elderly residents because of a failure of heating systems in mid-winter. Just as the job changes, so do the requirements of the Command Center, and this connection between location, role, and expectations must be clearly understood by any Emergency Manager involved in its design.

It must also be understood that not all emergency situations are predictable, and that any good Command Center's design must make it sufficiently flexible and adaptable to address a variety of circumstances, including those which may be unforeseen at the time that the Center is designed and built. Such facilities must be, to some degree, organic in their design; able to adapt and change with each new challenge in responding to emergencies. While the basic design will have specific parameters and expectations, changes in circumstances, roles, and technologies will occur, and these too will need to be incorporated into the design.

As recently as the 2000s, many hospitals and other facilities continued to rely on pagers for staff recall and overhead paging systems for internal communications. In this era of the nearly universal "smart phone" and ubiquitous tablet computers, offering such resources today would probably cause staff to question the knowledge and ability of the Emergency Manager! In truth, it is unlikely that any Emergency Manager operating in a healthcare facility at that time would have foreseen these developments, and yet, they MUST be accommodated. There is no doubt that similar changes in technology will continue to occur, and any Command Center design will require the ability to incorporate such changes as they occur.

Few specific resources exist which advise the Emergency Manager on the design of a Command Center, specifically for a healthcare facility. The vast majority of resources speak of an Emergency Operations Center (EOC), which is the increasingly common term for an emergency Command Center which serves a community, rather than a healthcare facility. Since it can be argued that any type of healthcare facility is, in fact, a specialized community, it is reasonable to draw from information on the design of community-based EOCs when considering the design of a Command Center for a healthcare facility. Indeed, such an approach can help to foster a basic ability to effectively integrate the facility's response to the crisis with that of the local community. However, one must never lose sight of the primary business of the healthcare-based Command Center and meeting the needs of both clinicians and clinical managers will need to be considered.

Student Projects

Student Project #1

Select a healthcare facility and determine its Command-and-Control model and methodology. Select potential locations for a primary and a backup Command Center. Consider the potential technological options to support a Command Center in each location. Consider all options, including cost. Prepare a proposal for the assignment of your selected space for the purpose of a Command Center in the event of an emergency, explaining and justifying your choices and decisions. Ensure that the report is fully cited and referenced, in order to demonstrate that the appropriate research has occurred.

Student Project #2

Meet with Information Technology personnel in order to fully understand the facility's existing computer network, its restrictions and its potentials. Conduct sufficient research to make yourself aware of currently available computer devices and technologies to support a Command Center operation in that facility. Consider all factors, including cost. Prepare a proposal for the acquisition and installation of a secondary computer network, aimed at supporting Command Center operations during and emergency, explaining and justifying your choices and decisions. Ensure that the report is fully cited and referenced, in order to demonstrate that the appropriate research has occurred.

Test Your Knowledge

Take your time. Read each question carefully and select the MOST CORRECT answer for each. The correct answers appear at the end of the section. If you score less than 80 percent (eight correct answers) you should re-read this chapter.

1. It has been said in emergency management circles, that the "currency" of disaster management is:

   (a) Funding
   (b) Staffing
   (c) Information
   (d) All of the above

2. In a healthcare facility, a Command Center's basic design may be described as:

   (a) Purpose-built
   (b) Improvised
   (c) Hybrid
   (d) All of the above

3. A Command Center assembly system in which all essential equipment is stored in kit form on secured carts which are taken to the required operating location when needed is called a:

   (a) "Pull" system
   (b) "Push" system
   (c) "Hybrid" system
   (d) "Purpose-built" system

4. When considering the ergonomics of a potential Command Center space, the Emergency Manager should always consider:

   (a) Lighting
   (b) Heating/Air Exchange
   (c) Ambient Noise
   (d) All of the above

5. In healthcare settings, the most common physical layout used for Command Center designs is the:

   (a) "Boardroom"
   (b) "Marketplace"

(c) "Bull's Eye"

(d) "Mission Control"

6. When planning to dynamically monitor news broadcasts as a Command Center function, it is essential that the placement of such equipment considers the problem of:

(a) Emergency power availability

(b) Generation of ambient noise

(c) Trip hazards due to cabling

(d) All of the above

7. No telephone operating in a Command Center should ever be equipped with voice mail because:

(a) Critical information can be lost/delayed

(b) Callers dislike voice mail

(c) Local legislation prohibits it

(d) All of the above

8. When considering the acquisition of computers and peripherals for the Command Center, it is best that such equipment should be:

(a) Dedicated to the Command Center

(b) Drawn from surplus equipment which is approaching obsolescence

(c) Multipurpose and in daily use

(d) Drawn from the equipment normally in the Business Office

9. When considering technologies for use in the Command Center, it is important to try to ensure:

(a) Multiple layers of redundancy, as a general principle

(b) Backup systems which are technologically independent of primaries

(c) The availability of older, more reliable technologies

(d) Both (a) and (b)

10. When creating a network, each potential operating site should be supported by a wireless router which:

(a) Is capable of supporting all of the devices in the room
(b) Is connected to an emergency power supply
(c) Is connected to the Internet Service Provider's network
(d) All of the above

Answers

1. (c)   2. (d)   3. (b)   4. (d)   5. (a)
6. (b)   7. (a)   8. (c)   9. (d)   10. (d)

Additional Reading

The author recommends the following exceptionally good titles as supplemental readings, which will help to enhance the student's knowledge of those topics covered in this chapter:

Emergency Medical Services Authority, California. 2006. Hospital Incident Command System Guidebook, pp. 55, .pdf document, https://adacounty .id.gov/Portals/Accem/Doc/PDF/hicsguidebook.pdf (accessed March 28, 2015).

Emergency Operations Center Planning and Design. 2008. U.S. Defense Department .pdf Document, www.wbdg.org/ccb/DOD/UFC/ufc_4_141_04. pdf (accessed May 05, 2016).

Fagel, MJ. 2010. Principles of Emergency Management and Emergency Operations Centers (EOC) (Google eBook), CRC Press, Boca Raton, FL, ISBN: 1439838526, 9781439838525

FCC/FEMA Tips for Communicating During an Emergency, FEMA/FCC webpage, http://www.fcc.gov/emergency-communications-tips (accessed March 27, 2015).

Joint Commission Resources. 2002. "Guide to Emergency Management Planning in Healthcare", Joint Commission on Accreditation of Healthcare Organizations, ISBN: 0866887555, 9780866887557

Rapp RR. 2011. Disaster Recovery Project Management: Bringing Order from Chaos, Purdue University Press, ISBN – 9781557535887

CHAPTER 5

The Business Cycle and Documentation

Introduction

Every Command Center in any healthcare facility will have variations in its normal operations. These may be driven by the Command-and-Control model in use, by the content of the Emergency Response Plan, by the nature and characteristics of the emergency, or by the corporate culture. What each has in common is that any truly good and effective Command Center is not simply a reactive process, responding to each issue which arises. A truly effective Command Center should be, if not in the earliest stages, then eventually and as quickly as possible, truly pro-active; managing the emergency well enough that events begin to be anticipated, and contingency responses developed and arranged in advance by the Command Center Team. Any experienced Incident Manager will tell the student that any crisis which has already foreseen and has a plan for its resolution in place is no longer a crisis; it is simply another problem which must be addressed.

Similarly, with the Command Center at the heart of the healthcare facility's decision making during any emergency, and the central "clearinghouse" for information, staff and resources, its preparations for, decisions and actions will undoubtedly be subjected to some type of review, following the conclusion of the emergency. This may be a less formal internal review of events as a part of a quality improvement process, a more formal Coroner's Inquest or public inquiry, or even some sort of legal or civil challenge regarding performance and liability. In each case, the documentation of precisely what occurred and when may become absolutely critical, and its ongoing occurrence should be a central part of the activities of the Command Center Team.

The process for decision making must not only be organized, timely and appropriate; it must also APPEAR to be all of these things! Moreover, both information and actions are likely to be considered from the perspective of "if it isn't written down ... it didn't occur." Fortunately, if the documentation process is formalized in the Command Center, there is a "duty of completion," and, in most legal systems, such a duty virtually ensures that the documentation generated will be admissible in the review, regardless of the type of review in question. For these reasons, the decision-making process and the actions of the Command Center Team are an essential part of good practice, and they require an appropriate amount of the Emergency Manager's attention.

Learning Objectives

Upon completion of this chapter, the student should be able to describe the documentation processes which are associated with the operation of a Command Center during an emergency in any type of healthcare facility. They should be familiar with the Business Cycle process, the methods and tools required for the creation of an Incident Action Plan (IAP), the need to document all occurrences and decisions, and also resource and information requests, and how these were individually managed. The student should be familiar with progress reporting processes, such as the Situation Report, and with formal summaries of events upon the completion of the emergency response, such as After-Action Reports.

Business Cycle Process

The Command Team and the Business Cycle are the "heart and soul" of the response to any crisis in a healthcare facility

In any Command Center, the Business Cycle (sometimes in the United States called a "Planning Cycle"[1]) should be a documented, structured process by which those who are tasked with major roles in the management of the emergency will meet, together with the Incident Manager, in order to exchange and analyze information, facilitate the development of the IAP,[2] to receive assignments from the Incident Manager, and to report on progress and problems encountered.

The structure of the Command Team will be dictated by which variant of the Incident Command System[3] the Team is using, although healthcare settings typically use a specific variant, such as HEICS[4] or Healthcare Emergency Command and Control System (HECCS). Each member of the Command Team will fill one of the key roles, whether as part of a preassigned response, or on an ad-hoc assignment from the Incident Manager.

All meetings will occur in the facility's Command Center. In most circumstances, the Command Team will not meet continuously; after the initial meeting, they will gather periodically, on a schedule determined by the Incident Manager and based upon the current requirements of the incident and the organization, usually once in each Operational Period. At each of these meetings, the current status of the incident and the problems encountered will be reported to the group, and the group members will themselves be expected to report on their own progress. The group will work collectively on determining the goals and objectives to recommend to the Incident Manager; in essence, the "next steps" at each stage of the incident management process. Finally, they will receive additional assignments, where appropriate, and a meeting time for the next meeting.

When circumstances dictate, the Incident Manager may alter the frequency of the Business Cycle meetings, increasing or decreasing the length of the Operational Period,[5] based upon the best assessment of the current situation, the identification of new "needs" by those in the field, or a need to reassess the current situation and develop and implement new strategies and objectives. All such meetings will be formal and minute-ed, and chaired by the Incident Manager. All reports, information requests, and resource requests will be logged and assigned to one or more individual team members, and then monitored and tracked for completion. The Incident Manager will be responsible for the completion of the Event

Log, and the reporting of incident progress, as appropriate, by means of the Situation Report, and should be supported in these efforts by one or more Scribes.

Immediately upon the completion of the incident, the Incident Manager will hold a final Business Cycle meeting. This will occur in order to obtain final reports and perform a final debriefing of all of the members of the Command Team. All documentation related to the incident will be gathered and collated, and a debriefing of other staff involved in the incident will be staged, if required. The documentation will be used by the Incident Manager, often assisted by the Planning Lead and the Scribe(s), to create a final report on the incident and its response, along with any recommendations for changes and improvements to future responses, normally called an "After Action Report."[6] This document can be circulated to all senior decision makers, and to others, as dictated by individual corporate policy. The After-Action Report, along with all of the documentation collected, and the Event Log, are then sealed and sent for long-term secure storage. In healthcare organizations, this occurs most typically in either in the files of the Incident Manager, or in corporate Risk Management or the organization's legal department.

The processes described here are essential to the management of the incident. Each measure described contributes to the provision of a formal, structured process for the gathering and analysis of data, and for decision making. The in-depth documentation provides a permanent record of all decisions and actions, and the exact context in which they occurred. Without such a process, months later, the reason why a particular decision occurred at a particular time may be less clear, and therefore, subject to speculation after the fact. By documenting absolutely everything in this fashion, such speculation can be effectively eliminated.

By having both a "duty of completion"[7] and by completing all of the documentation at the time of occurrence, the use of such comprehensive documentation during any external review or legal action, while not automatic in all jurisdictions, is extremely likely to be permitted. To clarify, while this completion is not specifically a legal duty (e.g., specified by a special item of legislation), it is regarded (or can be argued to be) in most legal systems as a legitimate expectation of the "average, reasonable," organization upon its employees or those mandated by the employer with the operation of the Command Center, and therefore admissible in most courts, on a similar basis to either Nurse's Notes, or the notes created in a Police Officer's memo book.

Incident Action Planning Process

The IAP is an essential document for the effective management of any type of major emergency situation. Without a plan, the Incident Manager will be doomed to managing the incident almost exclusively by reaction and will be unlikely to achieve a position of pro-active response. Such a process permits the Incident Manager to organize both issues requiring resolution and resources, create and test strategies, communicate those strategies to the other members of the Command Team, and begin to manage by objectives. Management by Objectives[8] should be a central component of the IAP. An IAP formally documents incident goals, operational period objectives, and the response strategy defined by incident command during response planning,[9] and the management of the incident itself can be seen as project, and therefore subject to the principles of Project Management, and an exercise in Management by Objectives.

The earliest stages of the IAP will probably exist nowhere other than in the mind of the Incident Manager. This reality ensures that action to resolve the incident begins to occur quickly, because until the intervention process begins, the incident itself will continue to grow and develop, and the situation is likely to continue to worsen, affecting more people and becoming more complex. No two IAPs will EVER be exactly alike, although many may be similar, at least in terms of subject headings. Each IAP will vary in content, according to both the nature and the needs of the incident which is occurring. There is, however, a process to this plan development, and a number of action steps which should occur.

Assembling the Team

The Incident Manager will make a decision to activate the Command Center and will issue direction for this to occur. This should include the summoning of the Command Team, and often, the actual assembly of the Command Center at a designated location. In most healthcare facilities, there should be a preidentified group of individuals, including both primary members and designated "back-ups" who make up the Command Team for the organization. Such individuals are usually selected, based upon training, skill sets, or roles within the organization. It should be noted, however, that such individuals may not be readily available 24 hours per day, and so, these positions may require filling on an "ad-hoc" basis by other staff members, until such time as the predesignated Team Members can arrive to relieve them. In such cases, these individuals will lack experience in this type of operation, and will require briefing, close support and supervision, and the use of tools such as the Job Action Sheet checklists,[10] previously described, to support them.

Precisely who will be summoned can vary somewhat, based upon which Command-and-Control model the individual facility involved has incorporated into their Emergency Response Plan. In some Command-and-Control models (e.g., HEICS), all members of the Command Team are automatically activated, whereas in other (e.g., HECCS), only those Team Members who, in the opinion of the Incident Manager, are actually required to manage the incident effectively, will be summoned. Once the estimated time of arrival for each member has been identified, and time for the first Business Cycle Meeting can be determined and announced.

Establish Initial Business Cycle/Planning Meeting

The first meeting of the Command Team should occur at the predesignated time, with the Command Center fully assembled. The Incident Manager should be prepared to brief all of the Command Team regarding the current situation, its impacts, actual and expected, upon the facility, and any problems currently being encountered, as well as identifying any problems with a real potential for occurrence. Roles are confirmed, and individuals assigned to develop as much information as possible from within the responsibilities of their particular role (e.g., Liaison seeks information from the incident scene through emergency responders, Operations checks the current status of the Emergency Room, Logistics checks staffing and resources on hand), being prepared to contribute to a much more comprehensive assessment of the situation and its potential impacts on the facility at the next Business Cycle meeting. This first meeting is intended to get everyone in place, with an understanding of their roles and expectations, and an initial understanding of the incident. At this point in large incidents, the Business Cycle meetings will probably occur frequently (e.g., every 30 minutes), but this will be determined by the Incident Manager.

Developing Situational Awareness

The best Command Team in the world cannot begin to plan and execute the response to an emergency until they have a reasonably accurate evaluation of precisely what the emergency is, and how it is operating. The first operation period will be directed at the gathering and analysis of as much information as can be obtained. This information should include the type of incident and the precise circumstances of its occurrence in this case. Information should also include any likely impacts and secondary problems which can be foreseen. Command Team staff should reach out to local Emergency Management, and to the emergency response services (Police, Fire, EMS), in order to identify precise circumstances, estimated patient and casualty loads, recommended precautions and safety procedures.

To illustrate, a train has derailed near town. Is it a passenger train or a freight train? If the train is a passenger train, how many victims are on board? How severe are the injuries, and how many are deceased? Are there any secondary victims who were not actually on the train? Is this going to require a mass-casualty incident response? Are the victims all coming to this facility, or will they be distributed to a group of facilities? What triage classifications will we be receiving? If it is a freight train, are there any hazardous materials on board? What types? Have they been specifically identified? Are they leaking? Are the train crew injured? Are there any patients, either train crew or responders who will require decontamination? Where will this occur? Where is the train, relative to the facility? Which way is the wind blowing? Are any areas being evacuated?

Next, a relatively complete picture of the facility's current status is also required. How many staff are currently on duty? Of what types? What are the current statuses of the Emergency Department, Operating Theaters, and Intensive Care? How many beds are currently available in the facility? How many patients could be discharged to provide space? Are there other facilities nearby, and what space do they have? Are they activating their Emergency Response Plans? Do we have ongoing contact arrangements in place with them? How will these arrangements work?

Analysis of the information gathered should be the next step. To continue with the example already described. Do we have sufficient staff to manage this incident already in place? What types of staff do we require? Why do we need them? How long will it take them to arrive here? Which currently offline services (e.g., Diagnostic Imaging, Laboratory, O.R.) do we need to reactivate? How many patients can we manage appropriately with the supplies that are currently on hand? For what items? Are we likely to be overwhelmed with new patients? With all of this information at hand, we are ready for the second Business Cycle meeting, which will focus upon developing a much more complete assessment of the incident itself, and of our likely role in the response to it. This will be used to formulate strategies for response to the impacts of the incident, to be implemented during the second Operational Period.

Definition of Management Strategy

Once the information collection and initial analysis have been completed, the Command Team can begin to formulate a formal Incident Management Strategy. How, in general terms, will the facility or the organization begin to respond to the event in question? This decision will ultimately be made by the Incident Manager, but with considerable consultation and input from all other members of the Command Team. At this point, it is realistic to begin to view the successful response to the effects of the incident as a project, and to begin to employ Project Management principles and skills. These will involve identifying the actual steps required to resolve the incident, and to also identify any preceding measures which are required in order to ensure their occurrence.

To illustrate, it is decided that the Operating Theaters will all be required to effectively manage the injuries, but it is currently 2 a.m., and these are currently dormant. This will require not only the activation of both surgeons and anesthetists but also nurses. The theaters are likely all ready for use (they are typically cleaned the night before to be ready for the first case each morning), but will require cleaning, following each case, and cleaning requires specially trained staff. Surgical instrumentation, medical gases, and medications will also be required; where are they kept and how do you access them at 2 a.m.? Finally, you will require additional nurses to staff the Recovery Area, a separate skill in its own right. Who will obtain each of these resources? How will it be obtained? How long will it take to get all of these resources in place?

What this example represents is a single management strategy; one of many that will be required in order to resolve the incident, and an entire list of tasks which will need to be performed, if that strategy is to function and become effective. It is not enough to simply announce that a given event must occur; it must be thought out in step-by-step detail, by either the Incident Manager or another member of the Command Team, if it is to become anything more than just an idea. The same is true for absolutely every strategy that the Command Team formulates; for unless the "loop is closed," strategies are truly little more than ideas.

The entire response process should ultimately be committed to paper, or at least, to a computer diagram. Since what is being described previously represents a single strategy, requiring both cause and effect processes, it would probably benefit from the employment of what is known in Project Management as an Ishikawa,[11] or "fishbone" diagram. This process starts with the required outcome; in this case, the activation of the Operating Theaters, and essentially, "reverse-engineers" the process leading to that outcome, identifying every essential step, so that it can be both assigned to someone as a task, and then monitored for completion. This technique can be applied by the Incident Manager and the Command Team to the entire IAP, or to each of its components, as required, and can provide a "roadmap" for both the subsequent actions of the Command Center, and the ultimate resolution of the incident.

Identifying Goals, Tactics, and Tasks

For the purposes of this discussion, it is appropriate to define goals as very large scale accomplishments directed at the response to or resolution of the incident. For example, the development of sufficient in-patient

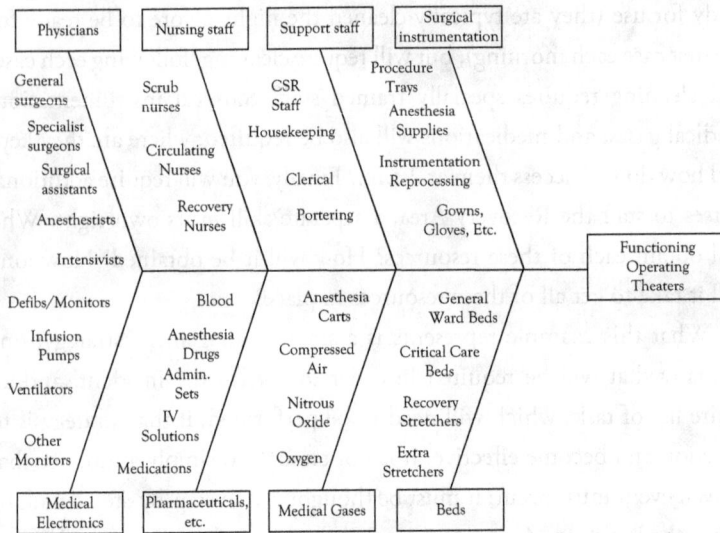

Figure 5.1 The Ishikawa diagram. A "fishbone" diagram for after-hours activation of Operating Theaters. These steps are by no means exhaustive

bed space to treat all of the victims of a mass casualty incident who require admission would represent a goal. A tactic might be described as a somewhat smaller scale event, one of several required to achieve a goal, but still significant in terms of resource usage. In the same context, a tactic might be the successful discharge of all in-patients for whom discharge is safe and appropriate. A task may be assigned a smaller scale event; one which is directed at supporting the completion of a tactic, or simply a requirement of the response to the crisis. To illustrate, in this context, a task might be the assembly and staffing of a "discharge lounge"; a holding area to which discharged patients are sent to await transportation, in order to clear the beds.

For planning purposes, the Incident Manager may employ the same Ishikawa diagram process previously described to identify, plot out, and assign each of the steps in the bed clearance process. In such a diagram, the goal would be the end product. Each of the arms would represent a tactic which is required in order to achieve the goal. The tasks are represented as incremental steps along each tactical "arm." In this manner, a template is developed for the achievement of specific major goals.

It is appropriate to point out here that it is entirely possible to complete much of this effort in advance, in some circumstances. This is particularly true for elements of the greater response to an emergency which are most likely to occur. These might include, but are by no means limited to:

- Preparation of the ER for a Mass Casualty Event
- Assembly of Decontamination Equipment
- Internal Surge Management Plan
- After-hours Activation of the Operating Theaters
- Emergency Bed Clearance
- Activation of the Command Center

Each of these "goals" can be developed in advance by the Emergency Manager, using the same type of Ishikawa diagram, and then developed into actual procedures. Once the TEWT exercise for each has identified operating locations and resource requirements, these procedures can be developed, using a similar type of checklist to the Job Action Sheets, which should be in use in the Command Center. Such checklists could then be added to the Emergency Response Plan as Annexes and tested periodically as exercises or drills. This approach turns the infrequently performed procedures involved into a "standardized work" approach, such as those used in both Six Sigma and Lean, further adding to the effectiveness of the overall Emergency Response Plan. It also accelerates the facility's ability to respond to a crisis, since, with all of the conversion steps identified in advance and transformed into simple procedures, the Incident Manager and the Command Team can focus on "when" to take a step, and not have to waste time deciding "how" to do it!

Setting Goals, Objectives, and Timelines

Once the actual measures that are required in order to achieve the resolution of the incident, it is reasonable to organize these into the IAP. It must be remembered that even in emergency response, everything doesn't happen at once! The goals and objectives must be placed in some type of rational order, and those goals and objectives with associated interdependencies (e.g., you can't clear the ER until in-patient beds are made available) must be identified and placed in the correct order. Some estimate for the actual completion time for each step will also be required. The Ishikawa Diagrams for specific processes should be a part of the planning process; however, this process will also benefit from the use of another tool, the timeline. Once again, there are tools from mainstream Project Management, such as GANTT Charts, which can help to organize the entire project, the individual steps involved, and their interdependencies.

Setting Operational Periods

Once all of this information is gathered, it becomes practical to attempt to manage the incident in smaller time segments, through the use of the goals and objectives identified, and the timelines required for the completion of each. By assigning tasks with reasonable completion times, it becomes possible to actual measure and evaluation progress in the facility's response to the crisis. With a sense of what should be completed and when, the Incident Manager can identify specific intervals at which monitoring tasks for completion are appropriate. The time between such intervals may be identified as Operational Periods. Such tools also make reporting more manageable and understandable. To illustrate, as a statement of objectives in a report to senior management, it would be appropriate to say "during the next Operational Period, it is our intention to finally resolve the problem with…" The Operational Periods are likely to start out with a fixed duration but are likely to be changed at the direction of the Incident Manager, as changes to the incident and its response dictate.

Establishing the Business Cycle/Planning Meeting Timetable

With all of the individual tasks, tactics, and goals, their probable timelines and Operational Periods identified, it becomes possible to create a more organized and rational schedule for the meetings of the Command Team. These should be driven by the Operational Periods and will become a tool which brings all of the members of the Command Team together to report, identify progress, identify problems, engage in problem-solving discussions, and receive new assignments from the

Incident Manager. These meetings also become an essential tool for the Incident Manager, for use in measuring both progress and performance, and for the early identification and resolution of new problems. In using this method, both the Incident Manager and the Command Team are constantly provided with the best possible information with which to make decisions and plan further measures, if required.

The timing of such meetings, as previously stated, is usually driven by the length of the Operational Periods, which are, in turn, driven largely by the needs of the incident and the facility's response to it. To illustrate, in the earliest stages of a mass casualty incident, Business Cycle Meetings may need to occur every thirty minutes, whereas, in a pandemic scenario, the Business Cycle Meetings might be simply daily occurrences. Such timing is variable, and may change as needs change, so that as the same mass casualty incident winds down, for example, the response is organized and effective, and with less problems requiring resolution, the Operational Periods will simply grow longer, and the Business Cycle schedule will be adjusted accordingly. In all cases, the scheduling and duration of the Business Cycle meetings are at the discretion of the Incident Manager.

Monitoring for Completion

Each discreet task and strategy will require monitoring for completion by the Incident Manager. When this measure does not occur, it is common for tasks to be set to one side due to conflicting priorities, and never returned to. When tasks are interdependent upon one another as components of a larger strategy, the effect of uncompleted tasks quickly becomes cumulative, and may, in fact, substantially degrade the entire response to the crisis, if the wrong tasks are missed, or a particular strategy fails. In order to monitor so many individual tasks and strategies, the Incident Manager will require help ... attempting to keep track of some many things at once in your head is a recipe for disaster, and any response process which is not documented in detail may be difficult to explain and defend, after the fact. Fortunately, there are, once again, extremely useful tools which can be borrowed by the Incident Manager from mainstream business concepts, which lend themselves extremely well to this task.

Using Mainstream Business Tools

Project Management

This process can be highly useful for most aspects of emergency management and guiding the facility through a crisis of any sort is no exception. It is entirely appropriate to view any major crisis in a healthcare facility as a complex challenge, with potentially dozens of interdependent tasks and measures required, and their successful completion is important. There is no need for the type of reactive management which has been common in most areas of emergency management, including that practiced in healthcare. A pro-active approach is typically far more successful, and certainly far less stressful for both the Incident Manager and the Command Team.

Many researchers tend to view crisis management as a necessary evil of organizational management.[12] However, by treating the resolution of the crisis as a "project" and applying the processes of project management to its analysis, organization of tasks, monitoring of tasks, and resolution of the incident, most issues will remain better organized, less will be forgotten or missed, the timelines for resolution are likely to be shortened, and the outcome is more likely to be successful. Interestingly, just as with the Command-and-Control models being proposed here, the majority of the clinical side of healthcare already works this way; they just don't call it project management! Think of a clinical emergency. A team of people assembles, they perform those interventions which are urgently required immediately, they then analyze what is happening, formulate a strategy for fixing it, set priorities for assessments, procedures, and so on, and, if the "project" is successful, the patient survives and recovers.

Many industries continually manage complex projects. Project Management is intended to identify and predict as many potential problems as possible, and to "plan, organize, and control activities,"[13] so that the project is completed successfully, despite potential risks which may have been present. Project Management is in use in a variety of sectors, including civil engineering and manufacturing, and there is no valid reason why this approach to structured problem solving and resource application cannot work successfully in emergency management for healthcare settings. While there is no shortage of "how to" books about this process, both in-person and online training and certification are also available from a variety of reputable sources, including both consulting firms[14] and universities.[15] As a result, most healthcare facilities would greatly benefit from having both an Emergency Manager and the group who are preselected for the Incident Manager role, to be formally trained in Project Management.

Ishikawa Diagrams

Also called "fishbone" or "cause and effect" diagrams were originally designed for the analysis of errors which had occurred in manufacturing processes. In a less conventional approach, this tool may also be used by the Incident Manager, or the Planning Lead, to map both the processes or tasks required to implement a specific strategy and also the resources that are required to support each process or task. Once the tasks and processes, and their required supports are identified, it becomes much easier to ensure that nothing has been overlooked, and to estimate the amount of time required in order to implement each, as well as for the implementation of the entire strategy which they describe. As such, the information generated can be used by the Incident Manager to develop and to drive the Business Cycle process, by helping to identify both the strategies required to support a particular response tactic, and also those resources which will be needed in order to support each tactic.

While such techniques can and should be valuable advance planning tools for the Emergency Manager developing response steps ahead of any emergency, they can also be an equally valuable tool for use by the Incident Manager in getting the response to the emergency properly organized, or for the analysis of some error or other issue in the response to the emergency. As such, this tool should be a part of the "toolkit" created by the Emergency Manager for use by the Incident Manager during any emergency. Such tools may be crude, blank templates, printed in advance and included in the toolkit, or may be computerized, using the basic software which should already be available in the Command Center, such as Microsoft Office. Excellent templates for such diagrams are readily available to download for free from various sources on the Internet,[16] and the student is encouraged to access these and practice using them.

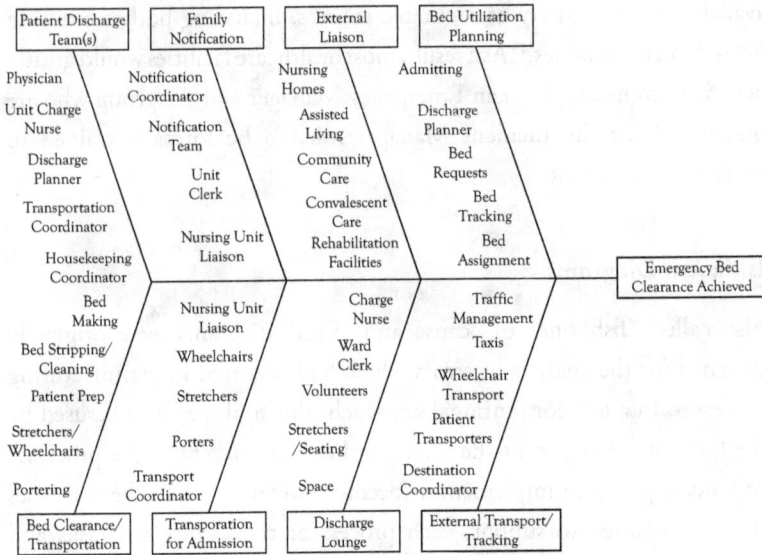

Figure 5.2 Emergency bed clearance. A "fishbone" diagram outlining resource requirements for an Emergency Bed Clearance Plan. The items are by no means exhaustive

Identifying and Implementing Support Tasks

The Ishikawa Diagram technique can help to provide the Incident Manager with lists of support requirements, whether these involve workspaces in which particular processes can occur, general or specialist staff, and the physical resources which they will require with which to perform the task in question. Such sites will require other support resources as well, including maintenance items, such as housekeeping, security, and resupply of expendable resources. With a complete picture of what is involved in the activation of a specific task needed to support a given strategy, that task can then be assigned for completion in support of the strategy, through the Command Center's Business Cycle meetings. The appropriate Ishikawa Diagram can be used to facilitate discussion, problem-solving and task assignment, as a part of the Business Cycle process. Much of this development can be effectively performed in advance, and formalized, using the Checklist process previously described. This balances the need to ensure that a task is performed thoroughly and correctly, without improvisation, against the need to expedite response to the crisis. Rather than having to provide the person who will implement the task in question with detailed, step-by-step verbal instructions, they can be simply handed the appropriate checklist and told to follow the steps and report back if there is a problem. Simply directing someone to perform a specific task and hoping that they "get it right" is rarely a formula for success.

(Insert Agency/Hospital Name)

Code Yellow, Amber, Black: Special Note A

Search Checklist – Nursing Departments

Date: _____   Unit: _____   Searched by: _____

Time Completed: _____   Time Delivered: _____

Assign someone to deliver completed checklist to the Code location

AREA	SEARCHED	COMMENTS
All Patient Rooms	☐	
Housekeeping Rooms	☐	
Dirty Utility Room	☐	
Clean Utility Room	☐	
Washrooms	☐	
Lounges	☐	
Kitchen	☐	
Nurses' Station	☐	
Med Room	☐	
Stairwells	☐	
Storage Rooms	☐	
Halls	☐	
Offices	☐	
Locked Rooms	☐	
Linen Room	☐	

Figure 5.3 A simple procedural checklist. A Checklist for the Search of a single Nursing Unit for a missing person or a suspicious package. Such tools can be used for many purposes and should be developed and tested in advance of any emergency

GANTT Charts

A Gantt chart, named for its creator, Henry Gantt, can be a useful tool for the Incident Manager to use for tracking both progress and timeliness of completion for both tasks and strategies. The Gantt chart displays activities such as tasks and strategies as blocks or bars over time.[17] As such, it displays the interconnectedness of multiple tasks with a project and can be used to display all tasks and strategies concurrently over time. Taking all of the required tasks and strategies, and their estimated timelines, and plotting these on a Gantt chart may help the Incident Manager to identify elements of interconnectivity that were not initially apparent and may also help to identify potential issues requiring resolution, prior to their actual occurrence.

Such a tool can tremendously facilitate discussion during the Business Cycle by simply displaying it on a whiteboard in the Command Center and referring to it during the meeting. This tool can contribute greatly to the development of proactivity in the management of whatever crisis is occurring. It can be used for both the management and oversight of specific elements of strategy, or it may be used to display all elements of the overall crisis response. Excellent templates for the creation of Gantt charts are readily available to the Emergency Manager from a variety of sources, including free online downloads.[18] Such charts can also be created using simple graph paper, or by using the Insert Table function in any version of Microsoft Word. These can be added to the "toolbox" of the Incident Manager from such sources by the Emergency Manager.

Measuring and Monitoring Progress

The use of the Gantt chart can provide the Incident Manager with an important visual reference source. Through the creation of specific timelines for various measures and a process for tracking these measures, the Incident Manager is provided with an "at-a-glance" information source which permits the monitoring of completion of specific measures, as well as whether or not that completion is occurring in a timely fashion. Delays are identified, and can be acted upon, in the very next Business Cycle meeting, thereby ensuring that the "loop"' is closed, and no measure which has been implemented is subsequently overlooked, resulting in problems in the response to the crisis.

Monitoring for Effectiveness

The Emergency Manager in a healthcare setting should understand that simply monitoring for completion and timeliness is insufficient. It is

Activities	OP-1	OP-2	OP-3	OP-4	OP-5	OP-6	OP-7	OP-8
Patient Discharge Teams (PDT) Activated	■							
Bed Clearance Teams Activated	■							
Liaison Begins Survey of Receiving Facilities	■	■						
Transport Teams Activated	■							
Transport Resources Assembled	■							
PDT Patient Survey		■	■					
Patient Prep Occurs		■	■					
Patient Requirements Arranged and in Place			■	■	■			
Families Notified			■	■				
Discharge Lounge Opened		■	■	■	■	■		
Transport to Discharge Lounge		■	■					
Bed Turnover Commences			■	■				
Bed Utilization Notified as Beds Become Available			■	■	■			
External Transport Arranged			■	■				
Transport Destinations Assigned				■	■			
Traffic Management in Place			■	■				
External Transport/Tracking Begins			■	■	■	■	■	
Family Reunification					■	■	■	
Transport for New Admissions Begins		■	■	■	■	■		
Resources Stand Down						■	■	■

Figure 5.4 A simple Gantt chart outlining the procedure and timelines for the implementation of the previously shown Emergency Bed Clearance Plan. The steps are by no means exhaustive

absolutely essential that the result of the assigned task also be monitored. If the assigned task fails to address the issue it was intended for, it must be subjected to analysis, problem-solving, and revision, or the effort has been wasted. This analysis and problem-solving are essential elements of the Command Center Business Cycle; it isn't just about what happened and when. An effective Business Cycle not only assigns response tasks and records events but it must also continue to analyze the event itself and the response tasks assigned to address it, in order to drive a process which generates both pro-activity and positive results.

The tools which have been previously discussed can be used as a part of the Business Cycle to organize tactics and assign tasks, to simplify and standardize emergency instructions, and can also be used to analyze results. They employ some of the best practices of Six Sigma and Lean for Healthcare to any emergency response, in order to make the Business Cycle a highly effective method for driving the resolution of the emergency with a process of continuous quality improvement. There was a time when the average Command Team would essentially sit in a room and respond to each bad thing as it happened. Through the efforts of the knowledgeable Emergency Manager to introduce these key business practices to the Command Center Business Cycle through advance preparation and Incident Manager training, that time has passed.

Documentation

The documentation of the response to whatever crisis has occurred is an essential part of the responsibilities associated with the Business Cycle and the Command Center. It has been said that "it is not enough to do the right thing ... one must be SEEN to do the right thing!" While this is certainly a true adage, in a healthcare setting, it is insufficient. In fact, one must not only be SEEN to do the right thing, but one must also be able to demonstrate this fact consistently and comprehensively, on paper, after the fact! Just as in every other aspect of the provision of healthcare, emergency management has an expectation of consistent and professional documentation, and this occurs in an environment in which the attitude in any type of review which occurs after the fact is likely to be "if it isn't written down ... it didn't happen!"

It is for these reasons that the Incident Manager and the Command Team have a Scribe attached to their operation. It is this individual's job to assist the Incident Manager in creating the most consistent and comprehensive documentation possible of the crisis response operation, at the time of occurrence, and with a duty of completion. This process helps to ensure that the information generated by the entire response, including each decision and step taken, how it was done and why it was necessary. These facts are necessary for later review, learning and improvement, and may actually be required in order to defend both the Incident Manager and the healthcare facility against assertions of inadequate or inappropriate responses in managing whatever crisis has occurred. Such documentation can also be essential in assisting a healthcare facility in achieving the recovery of some or all response costs from both insurance carriers or various levels of government, depending upon the type of administrative setting it is operating in.

It is equally important to standardize the process of documentation itself. In the rest of healthcare, and particularly in the clinical sector, absolutely everything done is documented, and it is done in a standardized format. Whichever physician or nurse has provided some service to a patient, it will be documented in the same manner on an identical form which is expressly designed for the purpose. There is a duty of completion, and virtually all of such forms are admissible, in fact will probably be subpoenaed, in any legal proceedings which may arise from the care of the patient. There is no reason why the expectation for emergency management in the healthcare setting should be any different.

The Emergency Manager who is operating in a healthcare setting must ensure in advance that there is not only an Emergency Response Plan, but that the Plan contains a package of standardized, easy to find and easy to use documents, for use in recording both events and decisions from the Business Cycle meetings, the formulation of strategies and the assignment of tasks, the receipt and filling of requests for both information and resources, and the outward and upward reporting of status and results, both during the incident and after the fact. Such documents must be readily available, and easy to use, and MUST be completed at the time of occurrence, since their later admissibility in an external review or a court proceeding may be crucial to defending the staff and the facility. The documentation of the Business Cycle is as important as the meetings themselves!

Job Action Sheets

These sheets provide consistent and standardized instructions to all essential personnel who are functioning in the Command Center and may be extended outward by the Emergency Manager to other essential functions. Each Job Action Sheet[19] is specific to the assigned role, and will provide clear, step-by-step instructions to the user. They are not comprehensive, and cannot be, due to the fact that each emergency event is different. They can, however, provide a set of standardized measures which MUST be taken by the incumbent in each role, regardless of the type of emergency which is operating. The steps are written in clear and unequivocal language; they are orders, not suggestions, and they are sequential. They may also be differentiated as Immediate, Intermediate, and Long-term actions. On a well-designed Job Action Sheet, the user will, as each measure is completed, note the time of completion and initial the entry. Once each Job Action Sheet is completed, it should be given to the Incident Manager for inclusion in the permanent record of the Command Center.

Such tools function as a reminder for those who are experienced in Command Center operations and their respective roles, and its directions will serve as a "roadmap" of sorts, for the inexperienced user. They are a tremendous tool for consistency in mounting the operation of the Command Center and the Business Cycle and a labor-saving device for the Incident Manager. If a given Job Action Sheet contains 40 step-by-step instructions for the user, those represent 40 elements of work direction that the Incident Manager will not have to remember, provide, or monitor for completion. Multiplied across the entire Command Center Team, the labor savings for the Incident Manager, and the amount of consistency and standardization generated are truly immense! The use of this tool can be extended to an entire range of emergency response functions, including other key roles, or the development of other key response resources (e.g., assembly of the Command Center, assembly of a Triage Area, and so on). In addition, the use of such tools, taken collectively, will provide a comprehensive, step-by-step chronology of every measure taken to prepare for the response to the emergency, and the duty of completion makes that information fully admissible in many court proceedings.

(Insert Hospital/Agency Name)
Emergency Response Plan Annex
Emergency Instructions

Job Action Sheet – Safety Officer

Function: (Occupational Health and Safety / Infection Prevention and Control / Risk)

Reports directly to the Incident Manager. Responsible for the safety of assigned staff for the duration of the emergency. Maintains authority to temporarily suspend any plan, procedure or strategy considered to be unsafe.

Completed by: _____   Unit: _____   Date: _____   Time: _____

1. This form is to be completed EVERY time that the appropriate Role is activated, or if you are asked to fill this Role on a temporary basis.
2. Complete each listed step in the order provided, until the Code is cancelled, or you are relieved by trained staff, or are directed to stop.
3. As each step is completed, note the time of completion in the appropriate box and initial in the box beside the time of completion.
4. All used forms, whether fully completed or not, are to be forwarded to the trained staff member who relieves you, or to the Incident Manager.
5. All used forms are to be immediately replaced from those available on the Intranet.

Upon Being Asked to Fill This Role:

Step #	Measure	Time	Initial
1	Review all of the steps in this Job Action Sheet. It will provide you with generic responsibilities and instructions.		
2	Review all of the steps in the appropriate Emergency Colour Code Annex. It will provide you with incident-specific responsibilities and instructions.		
3	If you have not been pre-designated for this role, be aware that there are pre-designated individuals to fill this role. If you are approached by one of these individuals, you are expected to transfer the role to that individual, brief them, and then follow instructions.		

Upon Activation of the Command Center (Immediate Measures)

Step #	Measure	Time	Initial
4	Assess and anticipate unsafe situations.		
5	Develop and recommend measures for staff safety based on information provided.		
6	Evaluate need for equipment, supplies such as decontamination, isolation, personal protective (PPE).		
7	Be alert to any hazardous conditions throughout the facility.		
8	Review, tour and inspect work sites throughout the facility on an ongoing basis.		
9	Be prepared to temporarily stop work and / or prevent unsafe acts until safety conditions met.		

Date of Creation/Revision: (Insert Date)

Figure 5.5 The Job Action Sheet. A typical Job Action Sheet for the key role of Safety Officer. Note the clear step-by-step instructions and the "standardized work" approach. Developed in advance, such tools can save tremendous amounts of time and work during the crisis response

Intermediate Measures

Step #	Measure	Time	Initial
10	Review, investigate and respond to any Staff safety-related complaints throughout the facility.		
11	Investigate and document any incidents of job-related injury or illness.		
12	Liaise with Infection Prevention and Control as required.		
13	Provide required information to Liaison for external agencies such as Public Health.		
14	Monitor safety conditions and develop measures to ensure the safety of all assigned staff throughout the emergency situation.		
15	Monitor efficacy of infection prevention and control measures. (incident dependent)		
16	Monitor efficacy of decontamination procedures. (incident dependent)		
17	Evaluate need for additional equipment and communicate need to Logistics as required.		
18	Ensure that the Incident Manager is continuously aware of your activities and results.		

Long-Term Measures

Step #	Measure	Time	Initial
19	Observe all staff and volunteers for signs of stress and inappropriate behavior.		
20	Ensure that staff is provided with appropriate rest and respite as required.		
21	Complete all required documentation and provide to the Incident Manager, prior to standing down.		
22	Stand down your role, when advised by the Incident Manager that it is no longer required.		

1. Return completed forms immediately to (insert location).
2. All completed forms must be received within 8 hours of the conclusion of the incident.
3. Ensure that the used form is replaced in the Emergency Response Plan binder, by printing a replacement form from the Intranet.

Date of Creation/Revision: (Insert Date)

Figure 5.5 (Continued)

Event Log

The Event Log is used to document all activities, problems, requests, decisions, strategies, and assignments associated with the response to the emergency event. It should be commenced as soon as practical following the start of the emergency, and certainly upon the activation of the Command Center. It can be used to document the arrival and departure of staff, changes of shift and responsibilities, major occurrences, and the minutes of each Business Cycle meeting. It should provide a straightforward, chronological narrative of the entire response to the emergency, in detail. Each new page used should be numbered sequentially, to provide for continuity, and to eliminate any potential for "missing" entries. The Event Log should also record the creation and completion/return of every other document used as part of the Command Center and Business Cycle processes. The person reporting will normally be either the Incident Manager or the Scribe, but in all cases, whoever is reporting should be clearly identified, typically with initials or a signature, and the time of each entry in the Event Log should be noted, as well.

The process of completion is not unlike the Nurse's Notes format, which is typically used by clinicians, and the duty of completion of the Event Log provides some degree of assurance that it will probably be admissible in subsequent inquiries or legal actions, following the conclusion of the emergency. By recording the creation and the completion/return of all other documents in the Event Log should also provide sufficient "connection" to assure their admissibility, as well. The Event Log will clearly identify exactly who did what, and when. It will also document all decisions, and the rationale for specific action and management choices by the Incident Manager and other members of the Command Team. The document provides comprehensive overview of all aspects of the Business Cycle of the Command Center and may also help to facilitate the upward and outward reporting functions required by the Incident Manager. Blank copies of the basic document should be readily available within the facility's Command Center assembly kit.

Resource/Information Requests

The information flow within a Command Center can be confusing at times, even with a well-organized and well-run Business Cycle. The requests for information and resources are likely to flow to the Command Center from various sources and will not always be received by the individual who will ultimately be responsible for the filling of the request. Additionally, a request may initially seem complete, but may ultimately require follow up for additional information or clarification on what is actually being specifically requested.

(Insert Organization/Hospital Name)

Command Center

Event Log Sheet

Incident: _____   Date: _____

Operating Site: _____

Time	Comments

Page ____ of ____

Figure 5.6 The Event Log Sheet. A fairly typical blank Event Log sheet. Note the timing required for each entry, and the provision for the sequential numbering of the sheets which will make up the total Log document

In a crisis management environment, it is surprisingly easy for requests to be set down somewhere, and then completely forgotten about, as the competing and conflicting demands of the incident intervene. If that is not enough, a great many of the requests received may have a monetary value associated with them, as resources may require purchase, or additional staff will definitely require payment, and so, documentation from beginning to end of any request with any economic impact is definitely required, particularly in environments in which healthcare facilities hope to be reimbursed for unscheduled emergency response expenditures by either insurers or various levels of government, depending upon the care model which is operating. Any effective Command Center, and its Business Cycle, require an information and request management system in which absolutely everything is tracked, and which "closes the loop" on the filling of requests of all types, as efficiently as possible.

The Information/Resource Request Tracking Form can provide a useful tool for the filling of all of these requirements. The requestor calls in to the Command Center, specifies what they need, and information is gathered on when the request was received, by whom, the identity and contact information of the requestor, where they are located, what they need, by when, and why. The information is then recorded and "triaged" to the individual who will be responsible for filling the request, and that individual's identity, role, location, and contact information, the time of assignment and the time of expected completion will also be recorded.

The request will then be entered into the Event Log, and also into the request tracking process. While many systems may rely solely on paper, the better-designed Command Centers will typically employ a dedicated whiteboard to the purpose of request tracking. In such cases, the information on the form is entered on the whiteboard, where it will remain until the request, whatever it may be, has been filled, or until a decision has been made not to fill the request for various reasons, and this information has been returned to the requestor. Command Center staff, and the Incident Manager in particular, can then use the whiteboard to monitor each request for timely completion, and to ensure that nothing is overlooked.

Situation Report[20]

This document is a formal periodic report of the progress being made in responding to the incident, as well as any problems encountered. This report is typically created by the Incident Manager, supported by the Scribe, and, in some models, by the Planning function. The intent is to provide for the type of upward reporting required to keep senior

(Insert Client Name) _____   EMERGENCY PLAN COMMITTEE

(Insert Organization/Hospital Name)

Command Centre

Resource/Information Request Tracking Sheet

Date	Time	Requested By:		Contact Number:	Location:

Item Required:		Quantity:	Deadline:	Reason Required:	

Request Rec'd By:	Contact Number:		Request Referred To:	Contact Number:

Request Filled:

Date:	Time:	Filled By:		Contact Number:	Delivery Confirmed

Request Declined:

Date:	Time:	Declined By:	Contact Number:	Reason:	

Finance Referral:

Date:	Time:	Referred To:	Contact Number:	Cost of Request:	Cost Center:

Figure 5.7 Information/Resource Request Form. A typical Information/ Resource Request Tracking Form. Such documents contribute greatly to the monitoring and closing of requests of various types and should be a mandatory part of every Command Center toolkit

management aware of what is occurring in the emergency response, and also to provide outward reporting to other agencies involved in the response, in order to supplement the efforts of the Liaison function in ensuring that all responders and various levels of government have appropriate access to the required information. Such reports are typically created and issued at the conclusion of each Business Cycle meeting, when the organizations' information is the most current, and when resource and support needed requests can be fulfilled in as timely a manner as possible.

Command Center
Situation Report

From: _____   Site: _____

Date : _____   Time: _____

CURRENT STATUS (ORGANIZATION):

CURRENT STATUS (EVENT):

SERVICE PROVISION:

Figure 5.8 The Situation Report. A typical Situation Report form.
Note the different headings provided to ensure consistent information
and progress reporting. Such blank forms should be a part of every
Command Center toolkit

UNRESOLVED ISSUES:

COMING EVENTS:

WEATHER FORECAST:

SUMMARY:

Time of Next Report: _____

For Further Information Contact:_____

Figure 5.8 (Continued)

Deciding to Stand Down

In any emergency involving a healthcare facility, the decision to stand down from the emergency response is typically made collectively, and not unilaterally. There are many aspects of the response in which the decision to stand down can potentially affect clinical outcomes, and so, input from all sources, with the final decision being made by senior management, is the most likely scenario. That being said, the information and tracking generated by the Command Center staff and by the Business Cycle itself are likely to play a key role. With the Command Center tracking all resource requests and response activities through the Business Cycle, it is likely that this information will provide the first cues that the need for special response to what is happening is winding down.

It is likely that the first sign will be a decrease in information or resource requests, or that such requests begin to change in nature, from the gathering of information and resources to manage the crisis, to the gathering of information and resources on managing a patient load which has become more "static." Care is a continuum, and such information as the fact that EMS at the scene is advising that all victims have been transported, or the temporary treatment area is no longer required, or that the Emergency Department is re-stocking, after being overwhelmed, or that the current backlog of patients in the process are waiting for the Operating Theaters or stuck in Recovery, awaiting in-patient beds.

While such changes will not necessarily generate a complete stand-down, it is likely to result in discussions during Business Cycle meetings about phasing out "front-end" crisis services, such as an overstaffed Emergency Department or temporary treatment areas, in order to re-focus the existing resources on assisting other services, further along the continuum of care, which are still overwhelmed. Finally, the surge in demand for services will reach the point at which crisis response is no longer required, and the Command Center and its Business Cycle can focus on the development of activities which are directed at permitting the entire organization to begin an actual recovery from the crisis.

It is not until the Business Cycle relates that most of the recovery activities are in place, with staff rotated and rested and re-supply of all areas occurring, that the time has probably come to stand down the emergency response and return to normal operations. At that point, the Incident Manager will stage a final Business Cycle meeting, receiving final reports, collecting all documentation, and thanking and releasing all Command Team members and support staff. A final Situation Report will be issued to all outside agencies which have received updates throughout the emergency response. The facility will be advised that the emergency response has ended, and that normal operations have resumed. The Command Center will be refurbished and re-stocked, then disassembled and repacked, ready for the next emergency. The Incident Manager will then close out the Event Log and begin the next steps in the recovery process.

With the Command Center closed down and returned to storage, the Incident Manager must begin to analyze what has happened. This will include an early and comprehensive debriefing of all staff who participated in the emergency, either in the Command Center or on the "front lines," in order to gather as much information from them regarding what went well and where opportunities for improvement exist. The next stage is the detailed review and analysis of all of the documentation generated by the emergency, including the Job Action Sheets, the Event Log, Information/ Resource Request Tracking forms, and the Situation Reports which were issued. With this information in hand, the Incident Manager is ready to begin to write the After-Action Report.

After-Action Report

This report is generated at the conclusion of the incident and is normally crafted by the Incident Manager(s), usually assisted by the Scribe(s), the Emergency Manager, and any personnel assigned to the Planning function. It is intended to provide a clear and succinct description of the emergency which occurred, the impacts on the healthcare facility, and the strategies, tactics, and tasks required to permit the appropriate response of the facility to the situation. It should identify problems encountered and how these were managed, along with specific recommendations for the improvement of future responses. The After-Action Report should also recognize and report all successes and should acknowledge and thank those responsible for these. Finally, with the assistance of the Finance function, it should provide a summary of costs, describing in detail the expenses incurred as a result of the response, in case there is any possibility of financial compensation from outside sources.

This document, when completed, will be sent to the senior management team of the facility, ideally within seven working days of the conclusion of the incident. It can also be used for insurance claims and for future training endeavors. Finally, a copy of the After-Action Report should be packaged, along with ALL of the documentation generated by the incident response, including the Job Action Sheets, the Event Log, Information/Resource Request Tracking Sheets, and the Situation Reports, and should be sealed and delivered to the appropriate location within the organization for long-term, secure storage, against future need.

This location will vary by organization, but is most likely to be the Legal Department, Risk Management, or the Emergency Manager.

Conclusion

The response to a crisis is NOT "business as usual," even in a healthcare facility, where the management of crises are a part of the everyday job description. If normal procedures and methods worked in emergency response, there would be no emergency to respond to. The Command Center and the Business Cycle provide an essential construct in which to engage in "outside the box" thinking and a unique, collaborative, and creative problem-solving process with which to manage the response to an emergency of any type. The "heart and soul" of this process is the Business Cycle. It permits a team (or teams) of people, who may not even work closely on a daily basis, to work collaboratively, in an atmosphere of cooperation and trust, to find strategies, tactics, and tasks with which to effectively manage an abnormal incident, and then to successfully implement these measures, in order to effectively guide the organization to the other side of the emergency event as effectively as possible.

The skills and information described in this chapter are essential knowledge for any Emergency Manager working in a healthcare setting. They provide a "toolkit" of both documents and mainstream business management techniques and methods drawn from such models as Project Management, Lean for Healthcare, Six Sigma, and Continuous Quality Improvement. Such powerful tools will nearly always prove to be useful to the practice of emergency management within the healthcare setting, whether in the day-to-day planning, education and training, or mitigation processes, or when an actual major emergency challenges both the Emergency Manager and the facility itself.

Student Projects

Student Project #1

The student will select a single, discreet, major task which may be required in order for the facility to successfully respond to a major emergency (e.g., assembly of decontamination equipment). Talk to those responsible for the equipment, establish what the current procedures are, and identify any problems which have already been identified. Next, conduct research and identify how this procedure is managed in other healthcare facilities elsewhere, as well as any problems which other facilities have encountered. Next, create an Ishikawa (fishbone) diagram, identifying all of the required steps required to successfully complete the procedure. Now create a step-by-step checklist for the completion of the procedure you are studying and test it if you can. Finally, create a report recommending the adoption of the procedure which you have created. Ensure that major points are accurate and factual, and are appropriately cited and referenced, in order to demonstrate that the appropriate research has occurred.

Student Project #2

The student will develop a Project Plan for the creation of a new Document Package for the Command Center of their facility. This Project Plan should include both an Ishikawa diagram and a GANTT chart for the project. The student will conduct research in order to determine how Command Center documentation occurs at other healthcare facilities. The student will then create a blank template for each type of Command Center document which they feel is required. Finally, the student will create a report recommending and arguing for the adoption of the package of blank Command Center documents which they have created, and for their adoption into the facility's Emergency Response Plan. Ensure that major points are accurate and factual, and are appropriately cited and referenced, in order to demonstrate that the appropriate research has occurred.

Test Your Knowledge

Take your time. Read each question carefully and select the MOST CORRECT answer for each. The correct answers appear at the end of the section. If you score less than 80 percent (eight correct answers) you should re-read this chapter.

1. A documented, structured process by which those who are tasked with major roles will meet, in order to exchange and analyze information, is called:

   (a) Operational Period
   (b) Goals and Objectives Meeting
   (c) Situation Report
   (d) Business Cycle Meeting

2. An essential document for the effective management of any type of major emergency situation is called the:

   (a) Incident Action Plan
   (b) Project Plan
   (c) Situation Report
   (d) Event Log

3. A planning tool which "reverse-engineers" the process leading to the completion of a major response tactic, identifying every essential step, so that it can be both assigned to someone as a task, and then monitored for completion, is called:

   (a) Project Plan
   (b) Ishikawa or "Fishbone" Diagram
   (c) GANTT Chart
   (d) PERT Chart

4. Once an essential element, such as a Command Center, has been created to aid in the facility's response to a crisis, its activation may be both formalized and made easier through the development of:

   (a) A Step-by-Step Checklist
   (b) An Ishikawa Diagram

(c) A Training Program

(d) Both (b) and (c)

5. The timing and the duration of any Command Center Business Cycle meeting is normally determined by:

(a) Corporate Policy

(b) The Needs of the Incident

(c) Decisions by the Incident Manager

(d) Both (b) and (c)

6. A formal periodic report of the progress being made in responding to the incident, as well as any problems encountered, is called:

(a) A Situation Report

(b) An After-Action Report

(c) A Job Action Sheet

(d) An Event Log

7. In order to ensure that documents associated with the Emergency Response Plan are used by staff during the response to any crisis, they must be:

(a) Easy to Understand

(b) Easy to Find

(c) Easy to Use

(d) All of the Above

8. One of the major purposes of the Business Cycle is to drive the response to the emergency through:

(a) The Use of Best Practices

(b) A Cycle of Continuous Quality Improvement

(c) The Use of Standard Operating Procedures

(d) The Use of Clinical Standards of Practice

9. In any crisis involving a healthcare setting, the decision to stand down is likely to occur jointly, involving the Command Center and:

(a) The Emergency Department
(b) The Legal Department
(c) The Senior Management Team
(d) Risk Management

10. An essential planning tool which can be used to illustrate the timing, duration, and interconnectivity between the tasks in a given response strategy is called a:

(a) PERT Chart
(b) Job Action Sheet
(c) GANTT Chart
(d) "Cause and Effect" Diagram

Answers

1. (d)   2. (a)   3. (b)   4. (a)   5. (d)
6. (a)   7. (d)   8. (b)   9. (c)   10. (c)

Additional Reading

The author recommends the following exceptionally good titles and websites as supplemental readings, which will help to enhance the student's knowledge of those topics, or provide free access to useful tools and methods which are covered in this chapter:

Canton LG. 2007. Emergency Management: Concepts and Strategies for Effective Programs, Hoboken, NJ: Wiley Publishing, ISBN: 978-0470119754

Fishbone Cause and Effect Diagram, Template.net Website, www.template.net/business/word-templates/fishbone-diagram-template/ (accessed January 07, 2016).

Free Gantt Chart Template, Office Timeline Website, www.officetimeline.com/timeline-templates/gantt-chart-download (accessed January 06, 2016).

Public Health Emergency. 2012. Medical Surge Capacity and Capability Handbook, United States Department of Health and Human Services, Washington, .pdf document, www.phe.gov/Preparedness/planning/mscc/handbook/Pages/default.aspx (accessed January 02, 2016).

Shirley D. 2011. Project Management for Healthcare, Boca Raton FL: CRC Press, ISBN: 978-1439819531

Conclusion

The use of a Command-and-Control model can greatly assist any hospital in the resolution of a crisis, whether large or small. Such a model can greatly assist with the establishment of clearly understood chains of command, internal work direction, and effective coordination and collaboration with both other healthcare organizations and other emergency response agencies in the community. That being said, such models must meet the specific needs of the healthcare organization, which may not be precisely identical to those of community agencies, and, in some respects, they are likely to be dramatically different. Hospitals and healthcare agencies have specific needs, which are driven by issues to which other community agencies are not subject, such as specific legislative mandates and accreditation standards. Each of these mandates and standards exists for a legitimate reason and must be respected. For these reasons, the "cookie-cutter" approach to Command-and-Control systems simply will not work satisfactorily in a healthcare setting.

Moreover, healthcare agencies of all types must be able to coordinate their plans and activities with those of the larger healthcare setting, the community, and those other agencies which serve the community during any crisis. Even in a purely internal crisis, no organization functions completely in a vacuum. For this reason, any Command-and-Control model used by a healthcare agency must always meet the specific needs of that agency but should also seek effective interagency communication and coordination as highly desirable secondary factors.

Specialized Command-and-Control models, such as Hospital Incident Command System or Healthcare Emergency Command and Control System, which are based directly on the Incident Command System and Incident Management System, respectively, have the potential to achieve all of the aforementioned goals. Each is capable of meeting the specific needs and operating realities of a hospital or healthcare agency, while specifically addressing interagency communication and coordination issues effectively. Each model has its specific strengths and weaknesses, and each will need to be examined by the Emergency Manager. In the end, the healthcare-based Emergency Manager must select a Command-and-Control model which will effectively and fully meet the specific needs and operating realities of the healthcare organization, while promoting interagency communication and coordination, and also satisfying both legislative mandates and accreditation requirements. The task is not a small one, but it IS essential.

While there are similarities between the practice of emergency management in a healthcare facility and a community, there are also differences which are striking. Healthcare facilities deal with emergencies of some scale on a daily basis, and the stakes are often higher than in the community. Providing ongoing care and safety to those who are almost always the most vulnerable people in a community requires a different focus. The differences are not always clinical, but the clinical component is, without doubt, critical to the practice of emergency management in a healthcare setting. One does not need to be a clinician to be an Emergency Manager in a healthcare setting; but it is important to have a detailed level of understanding of the context.

As has been previously stated, Emergency Managers are sophisticated generalists; they require some level of knowledge regarding many subjects. In a healthcare setting, that includes not only a reasonable understanding of the physical environment in which patients are cared for and how that operates, along with inherent strengths and weaknesses. They must also understand precisely how the emergency event generates risk, and how the community and other levels of government may respond to the emergency. Indeed, in a community of specialized knowledge, being a knowledgeable and sophisticated generalist may be the healthcare Emergency Manager's greatest strength, by becoming the point at which all of the bodies of specialized knowledge converge, and by being the translator who is capable of effectively communicating the knowledge, jargon, concern, and expectations of each group to the others.

Afterword

The practice of emergency management in a healthcare setting is a complex process. All of the skills and challenges of "mainstream" emergency management are also present in this setting, but there are important differences. While the "mainstream" Emergency Manager must prepare for the protection of a potentially vulnerable community, his or her counterpart, operating in a healthcare setting, is responsible for protecting what is arguably the largest concentration of truly vulnerable people within that same community. In the community at large, crisis requiring the attention of the Emergency Manager is a relatively infrequent occurrence, whereas, in the healthcare setting, although the crises are generally on a smaller scale, such as a missing patient, a suspicious package, or an angry and distraught individual, crises may occur several times per day. After all, healthcare facilities do tend to be in the business of crisis management.

In the public setting, an Emergency Manager tends to be not so much a specialist, but a sophisticated generalist, functioning in an environment of elected officials and municipal or government department heads. Each of these is an expert of sorts in the operations and services of their own departments, but who has limited experience in true crisis management. The mandate is to prepare a group of people, who, apart from the three emergency services (Police, Fire, Emergency Medical Services), are probably not all that familiar with crisis management processes, to manage an infrequently occurring crisis of some sort.

Normal, day-to-day procedures and resource levels may require modification, and a process of guidance from the operation of "business as usual" to "crisis response mode" and back again. The role of the Emergency Manager, in such settings, is not that of "specialist" so much as "sophisticated generalist"; someone who has a working knowledge of the various municipal or government departments, and whose job it is to create and manage a framework within which these individuals may cooperate and collaborate, even when they are unaccustomed to doing so on a daily basis, in order to manage and resolve whatever crisis has occurred.

In the healthcare setting, the Emergency Manager must also be a sophisticated generalist, but also a specialist of sorts, functioning in an intensely competitive environment of highly educated specialists, in which all procedures and services are driven by a combination of "best practice," research and patient outcome. Every single patient to whom services are provided is either the victim of a current crisis or is recovering from the effects of an earlier crisis, and whether or not the people in such an environment have considered this before, the entire facility and its core business are all, in some fashion, about preparedness, response, recovery, and mitigation!

In any crisis response, the scope of practice for medical and care professionals within healthcare facilities remains the same; what differs, is the scale of the operation. Frontline staff already know about crisis response procedures, but require guidance and advance planning, in order to be able to, without prior warning, suddenly manage a surge in demand, in which a normal week's worth of seriously and critically ill or injured individuals arrives on the doorstep of the hospital in perhaps as little as two hours, and they must be able to do so safely, appropriately, and defensibly. In a society which is litigious, and this tendency is constantly increasing, the entire practice of emergency management within a healthcare facility has, arguably, as much to do with the ability to demonstrate "due diligence" after the fact, as it does with crisis response procedures.

Moreover, with technologies and services which are constantly changing and improving, the Emergency Manager must compete with highly educated and motivated department heads for limited funding on every project which is being considered or undertaken. In this environment, every funding and service proposal reaching the desk of the Chief Executive Officer has very likely been carefully crafted by an acknowledged "expert" in their respective field and has usually been impeccably researched to support its position in every single argument. In this environment, nothing less is considered acceptable.

There can be real challenges for the Emergency Manager when competing with a new patient care technology or an expanded scope of diagnostic or care services for the funding required for something which "might never happen," and the Emergency Manager working in a healthcare environment clearly requires an expanded skill set which "levels the playing field." What is required is a move to a practice of emergency management which is increasingly research-based. The Emergency Manager must acquire and develop a working knowledge, and credentials, in both research skills and methodologies. In addition, the Emergency Manager in a healthcare setting can benefit tremendously from the acquisition of training in "mainstream" business techniques and skills. Any Emergency Manager, regardless of their location of practice can benefit from this expanded skill set, but in the healthcare setting, it is absolutely essential to successful practice.

The "mainstream" business techniques which have proven useful in emergency management include, but are not limited to, several internationally recognized processes. The first of these is the process of Project Management. By utilizing internationally recognized processes, such as Project Plans, "Ishikawa" or "Cause and Effect" diagrams, Gantt chart, and a "Critical Path" approach, complex projects such as the HIRA, the Emergency Response Plan, the development of critical response procedures, and the creation and staging of emergency exercises, become more efficient, effective, and manageable. These processes and associated techniques can even be applied to the operation of the Business Cycle of the healthcare facility's Command Center, with tremendous effect. For example, the use of both Gantt charts and Ishikawa diagrams can also be used to support the Incident Manager in the critical function of the monitoring of assignments for completion and actual progress throughout the Business Cycle, during the emergency itself.

The technique of "root-cause" or "failure-mode" analysis, which can be used to analyze past problems and hopefully, mitigate against their recurrence, also has a role to play in this setting. The use of such Project Management techniques as the Ishikawa diagram can also contribute to an effective analysis process. Such processes can be used during the Business Cycle to analyze problems which are occurring on an ongoing basis during any crisis. They are also highly effective, after the fact, in order to help determine what went wrong and why, so that procedures can be improved and mitigation measures put into place, so that the response to the next emergency is less problematic and more effective.

The use of the techniques of the concepts of Six Sigma and Lean for Healthcare can also be used to great effect in preparing for any type of crisis response. The application of the principles of Lean for Healthcare can be used to create an Emergency Response Plan in which information and required instructions are far easier to both find and understand, making it much more likely that procedures and instructions in the Plan will actually occur during the response to any emergency. The creation of predesigned Job Action Sheets as "standardized work" checklists, means that when a crisis does occur, the response will be predictable and correct, first time and every time, and that it will also be thoroughly and admissibly documented, within every branch of the organization. Together, these techniques can take the facility's Emergency Response Plan, in the minds of frontline staff, from a confusing document in which it is difficult to find anything, to a trusted resource, and a "toolkit" containing almost everything that might be needed, to be relied on in any type of emergency.

Of equal importance is the fact that the use of such "mainstream" business techniques can also forge an important link between the Emergency Manager and the Senior Management Team of any healthcare facility. Most healthcare administrators are trained in Business Administration; they are not, or only rarely, clinicians themselves. Their jobs, like that of the Emergency Manager, are, in each individual case, to both create and to operate the various aspects of the actual environment in which the clinicians work and provide their services. As such, almost all have had some level of prior exposure, including, in some cases, in-depth training, in the various "mainstream" business methods which have been proposed in this book as tools for the Emergency Manager. Information which has been prepared using these techniques will contain both familiarity and credibility for the target audience and will provide the input of the Emergency Manager with potentially far greater weight and influence in the management process.

The days of the Emergency Manager as a retired "Cold Warrior" have passed. Increasingly, instead of being trained on "short-courses" or drawn from the various emergency services, Emergency Managers are university-educated in their own specific discipline. Within healthcare, individuals used to become responsible for the Emergency Plan almost by accident, and in addition to a long list of "regular" duties! Today, the Emergency

Manager is increasingly recognized and respected as a professional, and as a subject-matter "expert," in many of the various fields in which they practice. The field will continue to grow and evolve, conducting research, reporting results, and no doubt, developing its own new body of knowledge and techniques in its own right.

The practice of emergency management within any type of healthcare setting is certainly no exception to this evolution of the field. In fact, in the right circumstances, it has a potential to provide some level of leadership to the rest of the profession. While the use of the mainstream business tools and techniques described in this book for use in the healthcare setting are beginning to occur in some locales, they should become standard practices. While obtaining the training required in these techniques will require a good deal of effort by the individual Emergency Manager (it should become a part of basic education), it is clearly worth doing. In doing so, the practice of emergency management, wherever it occurs, can potentially become more efficient, more effective, and more credible. Emergency Managers, within the healthcare setting and beyond, can evolve into respected and essential contributors to the management processes of all types of institutions and environments.

Notes

Chapter 1

1. Farazmand (2001).
2. Thomas and Phillips (2013).
3. Phillips and Phillips (2011).
4. Green (2001).
5. FEMA (2008).
6. Molino (2006).
7. Caroline, Elling, and Smith (2013).
8. Penuel, Statler, and Hagen (2013).
9. Moynihan (2009).
10. N.A. (2014).
11. Yates (1999).
12. Australian Fire and Emergency Service Authorities Council (2004).
13. FEMA (2011).
14. Bush (2003).
15. FEMA (2014).
16. FEMA (2011).
17. US FEMA (2008).
18. N.A. (2014).
19. Office of the Inspector General (1995).
20. Gray (2004).
21. The Civil Contingencies Act (2004).
22. Moore and Lakha (2007).
23. London Emergency Services Liaison Panel (2007).

Chapter 2

1. Pan American Health Organization (2000).
2. Joint Commission Resources (2002).
3. Sorenson et al (2011).

4. Joint Commission Resources (2012).

5. Nemeth (2013).

6. Mackby and Cornish (2008).

7. Islam and Ryan (2015).

8. National Health Service (2013).

9. ICS Canada (2012).

10. Reilly and Markenson (2011).

11. Department of Public Health (n.d.).

12. The Joint Commission (2012).

13. California Hospital Association (2011).

14. CHA (2014).

15. Koenig and Schultz (2009).

16. Marx, Hockberger, and Walls, eds (2009).

17. Health Department (2007).

18. OHA (2013).

Chapter 3

1. Purpura (2011).

2. Molino (2006).

3. AFAC (2013).

4. USHHS (2012).

5. Molino (2006).

6. Haddow, Bullock, and Coppola (2013).

7. Canton (2007).

8. Perry and Lindell (2006).

9. Murphy (1998).

10. Perry and Lindell (2006).

11. Molino (2006).

12. Molino (2006).

13. Lindell, Prater, and Perry (2006).

14. Canton (2007).

15. Okes (2009).

16. Rother and Shook (2003).

17. Molino (2006).

18. Molino (2006).

19. Lindell, Prater, and Perry (2006).

20. Information Resources Management Association (2011).

Chapter 4

1. Giordano and Spradley (2006).

2. Hogan (2007).

3. Powers and Daily (2010).

4. Johnson (2009).

5. Rapp (2011).

6. Powers and Daily (2010).

7. Fagel (2010).

8. Fagel (2010).

9. Emergency Operations Center Planning and Design (2008).

10. N.A. (2015).

11. Penuel, Statler and Hagen (2013).

12. Emergency Medical Services Authority (2006).

13. Joint Commission Resources (2002).

14. N.A. (2015).

15. N.A. (2015).

16. Joint Commission Resources (2004).

17. Nagelkerk (2005).

Chapter 5

1. Fay (2007).

2. Porter and the American Academy of Orthopedic Surgeons (2009).

3. American Academy of Orthopedic Surgeons (2001).

4. Veenema (2012).

5. Walsh and Christen (2010).

6. Canton (2007).

7. N.A. (2016).

8. Phelan (2011).

9. Public Health Emergency (2012).

10. FEMA (2005).

11. Munro (2003).

12. Shirley (2011).
13. Lock (2007).
14. N.A. (2016).
15. N.A. (2016).
16. N.A. (2016).
17. Langabeer (2007).
18. N.A. (2016).
19. Molino (2006).
20. Walsh and Christen (2010).

References

AFAC. 2013. *The Australian Inter-service Incident Management System*, 4th ed. Australian Fire and Emergency Services Authorities Council.

All ESF role descriptions are drawn from the FEMA National Preparedness Resource Library. www.fema.gov/national-preparedness-resource-library (accessed February 20, 2014).

Amateur Radio Emergency Service homepage. www.arrl.org/ares (accessed March 29, 2015).

American Academy of Orthopedic Surgeons. 2001. *Emergency Care and Transportation of the Sick and Injured*, p. 845. 8th ed. Burlington, VT: Jones and Bartlett Learning.

Australasian Fire and Emergency Service Authorities Council webpage. www.afac.com.au/ (accessed February 19, 2014).

Australian Fire and Emergency Service Authorities Council. 2004. *Australasian Inter-Service Incident Management System Manual*. Pdf document, http://training.fema.gov/EMIWeb/edu/docs/cem/Comparative%20EM%20-%20Session%2021%20-%20Handout%2021-1%20AIIMS%20Manual.pdf (accessed February 19, 2014).

Bush, G.W. 2003. *Homeland Security Presidential Directive #5*. White House, Washington. Pdf document, www.fas.org/irp/offdocs/nspd/hspd-5.html (accessed February 21, 2014).

California Hospital Association. 2011. *CHA NIMS Compliance Checklist*. Pdf document, www.calhospitalprepare.org/post/nims-implementation-objectives (accessed February 25, 2014).

Canton, L.G. 2007. *Emergency Management: Concepts and Strategies for Effective Programs*, p. 124. New York, NY: John Wiley & Sons.

Canton, L.G. 2007. *Emergency Management: Concepts and Strategies for Effective Programs*, p. 178. New York, NY: John Wiley & Sons.

Caroline, N., R. Elling, and M. Smith. 2013. *Emergency Care in the Streets*, p. 2199. 7th ed. Burlington, MA: Jones & Bartlett Learning.

CHA. 2014. *ICS/NIMS Online Training Course*. California Hospital Association website, www.calhospitalprepare.org/icsnims-online-course (accessed February 25, 2014).

Ciottone, G.R., P.D. Anderson, et al. 2006. *Disaster Medicine*, p. 212. Mosby Elsevier.

Department of Public Health. n.d. *Hospital Emergency Incident Command System: Basic HEICS*. State of Iowa Department of Public Health. Pdf document, www.uiowa.edu/~medtest2/heics/Basic%20HEICS%20Final.pdf   (accessed March 01, 2014).

Emergency Medical Services Authority, California. 2006. *Hospital Incident Command System Guidebook*, p. 55. Pdf document, https://adacounty.id.gov/Portals/Accem/Doc/PDF/hicsguidebook.pdf (accessed March 28, 2015).

Emergency Operations Center Planning and Design. 2008. *U.S. Defense Department*. Pdf Document, www.wbdg.org/ccb/DOD/UFC/ufc_4_141_04 .pdf (accessed May 05, 2016).

Fagel, M.J. 2010. *Principles of Emergency Management and Emergency Operations Centers (EOC) (Google eBook)*, p. 323. Boca Raton, FL: CRC Press.

Fagel, M.J. 2010. *Principles of Emergency Management and Emergency Operations Centers (EOC) (Google eBook)*, p. 289. Boca Raton, FL: CRC Press.

Farazmand, A. 2001. *Handbook of Crisis and Emergency Management*, p. 7. FL: Boca Raton.

Fay, J. 2007. *Encyclopedia of Security Management*, p. 94. Oxford, UK: Butterworth-Heinemann.

FCC/FEMA Tips for Communicating During an Emergency, FEMA/FCC webpage, www.fcc.gov/emergency-communications-tips (accessed March 27, 2015).

FEMA. 2005. *National Incident Management System, Continuing Education Series*, p. 19. Washington: U.S. Federal Emergency Management Agency, Google Book.

FEMA. 2008. *National Incident Management System*, p. 27. Washington, DC: U.S. Department of Homeland Security. Google e- Book.

FEMA. 2011. *The National Incident Management System: Overview, US Federal Emergency Management Administration*. Washington. Pdf document, www.fema.gov/media-library-data/20130726-1853-25045-0014/nims_overview.pdf (accessed February 21, 2014).

FEMA. 2011. *The National Incident Management System: Overview*. Washington: US Federal Emergency Management Administration. Pdf document, www.fema.gov/media-library-data/20130726-1853-25045-0014/nims_overview.pdf (accessed February 21, 2014).

FEMA. 2014. *National Incident Management System: Independent Study Course*. Emergency Management Institute, Distance Learning Course. http://training.fema.gov/IS/NIMS.aspx (accessed February 21, 2104).

Fishbone Cause and Effect Diagram. Template.net Website, www.template.net/business/word-templates/fishbone-diagram-template/ (accessed January 07, 2016).

Free Gantt Chart Template. Office Timeline Website, www.officetimeline.com/timeline-templates/gantt-chart-download (accessed January 06, 2016).

Gray, D. 2004. *BTEC National Public Services (Uniformed) Book 1*, p. 275. London: Heinemann Publishing.

Green, W.G. 2001. *Command and Control of Disaster Operations*, p. 9. Boca Raton, FL: Universal Publishers.

Haddow, G., J. Bullock, and D. Coppola. 2013. *Introduction to Emergency Management*, p. 380. 5th ed. New York, NY: Butterworth-Heinemann. ISBN: 9780124077843, eBook ISBN: 9780124104051

Health Department. 2007. *Hospital Incident Command System (HICS) Training*. State of Minnesota Health Department. Pdf document, www.health.state. mn.us/oep/training/bhpp/hicstrain.pdf (accessed March 01, 2014).

Hogan, D.E. 2007. *Disaster Medicine*, p. 210. 2nd ed. New York, NY: Wolters-Kluwer Health. ISBN: 9780781762625

ICS Canada. 2012. *Incident Command System Operational Description*, sec. 1.2.1.3. ICS Canada. Pdf document, www.icscanada.ca/images/upload/ ICS%20OPS%20Description2012.pdf (accessed February 28, 2014).

Information Resources Management Association. 2011. *Clinical Technologies: Concepts, Methodologies, Tools and Applications*, p. 476. Idea Group Incorporated.

Islam, T., and J. Ryan. 2015. *Hazard Mitigation in Emergency Management*, p. 61. Atlanta, GA: Butterworth-Heinemann.

Johnson, J.A. 2009. *Health Organizations: Theory, Behavior and Development*, p. 385. Sudbury, MA: Jones & Bartlett Publishers.

Joint Commission Resources. 2002. *Guide to Emergency Management Planning in Healthcare*, p. 166. Joint Commission on Accreditation of Healthcare Organizations.

Joint Commission Resources. 2004. *Environment of Care Handbook*, p. 62. Joint Commission on Accreditation of Healthcare Organizations.

Joint Commission Resources, ed. 2002. *Guide to Emergency Management Planning in Healthcare*, p. 138. Oakbrook Terrace, IL: The Joint Commission. www. worldcat.org/title/guide-to-emergency-management-planning-in-health-care/oclc/50418820 (accessed February 27, 2014).

Joint Commission Resources, ed. 2012. *Emergency Management in Healthcare*, p. 4. 2nd ed. Oakbrook Terrace, IL: The Joint Commission. http://books. google.ca/books?id=Zuj_-tiv9uwC&printsec=frontcover#v=onepage&q&f=f alse (accessed February 27, 2014).

Koenig, K.L., and C.H. Schultz. 2009. *Koenig and Schultz's Disaster Medicine: Comprehensive Principles and Practices*, p. 298. Cambridge University Press.

Langabeer, J.R. 2007. *Healthcare Operations Management: A Quantitative Approach to Business and Logistics*, p. 156. Burlington MA: Jones & Bartlett Learning.

Lindell, M.K., C. Prater, and R.W. Perry. 2006. *Wiley Pathways Introduction to Emergency Management*, p. 278. 1st ed. New York, NY: John Wiley & Sons.

Lindell, M.K., C. Prater, and R.W. Perry. 2006. *Wiley Pathways Introduction to Emergency Management*, p. 335. 1st ed. New York, NY: John Wiley & Sons.

Lock, D. 2007. *The Essentials of Project Management*, p. 1. Burlington VT: Gower Publishing.

London Emergency Services Liaison Panel. 2007. *LESLP Major Incident Procedure Manual*, sec. 6.2. London, UK: The Stationery Office.

Mackby, J., and P. Cornish. 2008. *U.S.-UK Nuclear Cooperation After 50 Years*, pp. 105. Washington, DC: Center for Strategic and International Studies.

Marx, J.A., R.S. Hockberger, and R.M. Walls, eds. 2009. *Rosen's Emergency Medicine: Concepts and Clinical Practice*, 8th Edition, p. 2488. New York, NY: WB Saunders.

Masters of Science in Project Management. Boston University Metropolitan College, Website, www.msmonline.bu.edu/lpppc-mspm/ (accessed January 06, 2016).

Molino, L.N. Sr. 2006. *Emergency Incident Management Systems: Fundamentals and Applications*, p. 142. Hoboken, NJ: John Wiley Publishing.

Molino, L.N., Sr. 2006. *Emergency Incident Management Systems: Fundamentals and Applications*, p. 233. Oxford, UK: John Wiley Publishing.

Molino, L.N., Sr. 2006. *Emergency Incident Management Systems: Fundamentals and Applications*, p. 16. New York, NY: John Wiley & Sons.

Molino, L.N., Sr. 2006. *Emergency Incident Management Systems, Fundamentals and Application*, p. 142. New York, NY: John Wiley & Sons.

Molino, L.N., Sr. 2006. *Emergency Incident Management Systems: Fundamentals and Applications*, p. 177. New York, NY: John Wiley & Sons.

Molino, L.N., Sr. 2006. *Emergency Incident Management Systems: Fundamentals and Applications*, p. 503. New York, NY: John Wiley & Sons.

Molino, L.N., Sr. 2006. *Emergency Incident Management Systems: Fundamentals and Applications*, p. 506. New York, NY: John Wiley & Sons.

Moore, T., and R. Lakha. 2007. *Tolley's Handbook of Disaster and Emergency Management*. London: Taylor and Francis.

Moynihan, D.P. 2009. "The Network Governance of Crisis Response: Case Studies of Incident Command Systems." *Journal of Public Administration Research and Theory* 19, no. 4, pp. 895–915. Pdf document, www.lafollette.wisc.edu/facultystaff/moynihan/JPART194.pdf (accessed February 17, 2014).

Munro, R.A. 2003. *Six Sigma for the Office*, p. 53. Milwaukee, WI: ASQ Quality Press.

Murphy, J. 1998. *Rapid Incident Command System*, p. 11. Philadelphia, PA: PennWell Books.

Nagelkerk, J. 2005. *Leadership and Nursing Care Management*, p. 148. St. Louis, MO: Saunders Elsevier.

National Health Service. 2013. *Core Standards for Emergency Preparedness, Response and Resiliency.* London: NHS Commissioning Board. www.england. nhs.uk/wp-content/uploads/2013/03/eprr-core-standards.pdf (accessed February 28, 2014).

Nemeth, C.P. 2013. *Homeland Security: An Introduction to Principles and Practice*, p. 242. 2nd ed. Boca Raton, FL: CRC Press.

Office of the Inspector General. 1995. "FEMA's Disaster Management Program: A Performance Audit After Hurricane Andrew." *US Government Report*, p. 52. Google Books http://books.google.ca/books?id=-zX4qTHW0QQC& pg=PA51&dq=Emergency+support+functions&hl=en&sa=X&ei=aGAIU6 zLGIGmyQHgiYHYBQ&ved=0CCwQ6AEwAA#v=onepage&q=Emergen cy%20support%20functions&f=false (accessed February 22, 2014).

OHA. 2013. *Emergency Management for Healthcare Certificate.* Toronto: Ontario Hospital Association. Pdf document, www.oha.com/Education/ ContinuingEducation/Documents/Final%20-%20Emergency%20 Management%20for%20Health%20Care%20Certificate%20brochure.pdf (accessed February 27, 2014).

Okes, D. 2009. *Root Cause Analysis: The Core of Problem Solving and Corrective Action*, p. 4. ASQ Quality Press.

Pan American Health Organization. 2000. *Natural Disasters: Protecting the Public's Health.* Washington DC: PAHO.

Penuel, B.K., M. Statler, and R. Hagen, eds. 2013. *The Encyclopedia of Crisis Management* 1, p. 341. London: Sage Publications.

Penuel, K.B., M. Statler, and R. Hagen. 2013. *Encyclopedia of Crisis Management* 1, p. 354. Thousand Oaks, CA: SAGE Publications.

Perry, R.W., and M.K. Lindell. 2006. *Wiley Pathways Emergency Planning*, p. 394. New York, NY: John Wiley & Sons.

Perry, R.W., and M.K. Lindell. 2006. *Wiley Pathways Emergency Planning*, p. 391. New York, NY: John Wiley & Sons.

Phelan, T.D. 2011. *Emergency Management and Tactical Response Operations: Bridging the Gap*, p. 67. Oxford, UK: Butterworth-Heinemann.

Phillips, B.D. and D.M. Neal. 2011. *Introduction to Emergency Management*, p. 254. Boca Raton, FL: CRC Press.

Porter, W., and the American Academy of Orthopedic Surgeons. 2009. *Preplanning for EMS*, p. 79. Burlington, VT: Jones and Bartlett Learning.

Powers, R., and E. Daily, eds. 2010. *International Disaster Nursing*, p. 174. Cambridge, UK: Cambridge University Press.

Project Management Training for Your Organization. Project Management Institute, Website, www.pmi.org/Business-Solutions/Talent-Management-Project-Management-Training.aspx (accessed January 06, 2016).

Public Health Emergency. 2012. *Medical Surge Capacity and Capability Handbook*. Appendix C. Washington: United States Department of Health and Human Services. Pdf document, www.phe.gov/Preparedness/planning/mscc/handbook/Pages/default.aspx (accessed January 02, 2016).

Purpura, P. 2011. *Terrorism and Homeland Security: An Introduction With Applications*, p. 257. Butterworth-Heinemann.

Radio Amateurs Emergency Network homepage. www.raynet-uk.net/ (accessed February 28, 2015).

Rapp, R.R. 2011. *Disaster Recovery Project Management: Bringing Order From Chaos*, p. 3. Purdue University Press.

Reilly, M.J., and D.S. Markenson. 2011. *Healthcare Emergency Management: Principles and Practice*, pp. 78–79. New York, NY: Jones and Bartlett Learning.

Rother, M., and J. Shook. 2003. *Learning to See: Value Stream Mapping to Add Value and Eliminate Muda*, p. 3. Lean Enterprise Institute.

Shirley, D. 2011. *Project Management for Healthcare*, p. 13. Boca Raton FL: CRC Press.

Sorensen, B.S., R.D. Zane, B.E. Wante, M.B. Rao, M. Bortolin, and G. Rockenschaub. 2011. *Hospital Emergency Response Checklist*. World Health Organization, Regional Office for Europe. www.euro.who.int/__data/assets/pdf_file/0020/148214/e95978.pdf (accessed February 27, 2014).

The Civil Contingencies Act. 2004. Government of the United Kingdom. www.legislation.gov.uk/ukpga/2004/36/contents (accessed February 22, 2014).

The Joint Commission. 2012. *Emergency Management, Joint Commission*. Pdf document, www.uhnj.org/mdstfweb/The_Joint_Commission/Emergency%20Management.pdf (accessed February 25, 2014).

Thomas, D.S.K., and B.D. Phillips. 2013. *Social Vulnerability to Disasters*, p. 9. 2nd ed. Boca Raton, FL: CRC Press.

US FEMA. 2008. *Emergency Support Function Annexes: Introduction*. Washington: United States Federal Emergency Management Agency. Pdf document, www.fema.gov/pdf/emergency/nrf/nrf-esf-intro.pdf (accessed February 2014).

USHHS. 2012. What IS an Incident Action Plan? Public Health Emergency website, operated by US Dept. of Health and Human Services, Washington, DC. www.phe.gov/Preparedness/planning/mscc/handbook/pages/appendixc.aspx (accessed March 07, 2014).

Veenema, T.G., ed. 2012. *Disaster Nursing and Preparedness for Chemical, Biological, and Radiological Terrorism, and Other Hazards*, p. 132. New York, NY: Springer.

Walsh, D.W., and H.T. Christen. 2010. *National Incident Management System: Principles and Practice*, p. 46. Burlington, VT: Jones and Bartlett Learning.

Walsh, D.W., and H.T. Christen. 2010. *National Incident Management System: Principles and Practice*, p. 126. Burlington, VT: Jones and Bartlett Learning.

What IS Duty? The Law Dictionary: Featuring Black's Law Dictionary Free Online Dictionary, 2nd ed. Online website, www.thelawdictionary.org/duty/ (accessed January 03, 2016).

Yates, J. 1999. "Improving the Management of Emergencies; Enhancing the ICS." *Australian Journal of Emergency Management*, Winter 1999, Mt. Macedon. www.em.gov.au/Documents/Improving_the_management_of_emergencies_ Enhancing_the_ICS.pdf (accessed February 20, 2014).

About the Author

Norman Ferrier has worked in various aspects of Canadian healthcare for more than 42 years, and for 32 of those years has focused increasingly on emergency planning for all types of healthcare facilities and organizations, across the entire continuum of healthcare. Norm holds a Master of Science degree in Emergency Planning and Disaster Management from the University of Hertfordshire, in the United Kingdom. He holds a Certificate in Healthcare Emergency Management from the Ontario Hospital Association and is a member of the Institute of Civil Protection and Emergency Management. Norm was the principal investigator for the Government of Canada's National Assessment of Emergency Planning in Canada's General Hospitals and was on the faculty of the Ontario Hospital Association, where he designed and taught courses related to emergency management for those who manage all aspects of healthcare, both across Canada, and beyond.

Norm was also the Chair of the team which re-standardized the Ontario Hospital Association's Standardized Emergency Colour Codes and co-authored the Ontario Hospital Association's Emergency Management Toolkit. He also created and introduced the Ontario Hospital Association's Certificate in Healthcare Emergency Management. Norm has been published and speaks internationally and is the author of another college/university textbook, Fundamentals of Emergency Management: Preparedness, published by Emond-Montgomery. Norm was the 2013 winner of the Canadian Emergency Management Award, presented at the World Conference on Disaster Management. He lives in Tavira, Portugal, where he operates an emergency management consulting practice, focused primarily, but not exclusively, on healthcare.

Index

OTHER TITLES IN THE HEALTHCARE MANAGEMENT COLLECTION

- *Emergency Management for Health Care, Volume I* by Norman Ferrier
- *Strategic Data Management for Successful Healthcare Outcomes* by Lakkaraju Hema
- *Improv to Improve Healthcare* by Candy Campbell
- *Integrated Delivery* by David Stehlik
- *Mastering Evaluation and Management Services in Healthcare* by Stacy Swartz
- *Lean Thinking for Emerging Healthcare Leaders* by Arnout Orelio
- *Process-Oriented Healthcare Management Systems* by Anita Edvinsson
- *Behind the Scenes of Health Care* by Hesston L. Johnson
- *Predictive Medicine* by Emmanuel Fombu
- *The DNA of Physician Leadership* by Myron J. Beard and Steve Quach
- *Management Skills for Clinicians, Volume II* by Linda R. LaGanga
- *Management Skills for Clinicians, Volume I* by Linda R. LaGanga

Concise and Applied Business Books

The Collection listed above is one of 30 business subject collections that Business Expert Press has grown to make BEP a premiere publisher of print and digital books. Our concise and applied books are for...

- Professionals and Practitioners
- Faculty who adopt our books for courses
- Librarians who know that BEP's Digital Libraries are a unique way to offer students ebooks to download, not restricted with any digital rights management
- Executive Training Course Leaders
- Business Seminar Organizers

Business Expert Press books are for anyone who needs to dig deeper on business ideas, goals, and solutions to everyday problems. Whether one print book, one ebook, or buying a digital library of 110 ebooks, we remain the affordable and smart way to be business smart. For more information, please visit www.businessexpertpress.com, or contact sales@businessexpertpress.com.